Higher Maintenance

Managing the Dragon that is Chronic Illness
Transcending Limiting Beliefs
And Finding Happiness in the Moment

Marianne Granger

BALBOA.
PRESS
A DIVISION OF HAY HOUSE

Balboa Press books may be ordered through booksellers or by contacting:

Balboa Press
A Division of Hay House
1663 Liberty Drive
Bloomington, IN 47403
www.balboapress.com
1 (877) 407-4847

Because of the dynamic nature of the Internet, any web addresses or links contained in this book may have changed since publication and may no longer be valid. The views expressed in this work are solely those of the author and do not necessarily reflect the views of the publisher, and the publisher hereby disclaims any responsibility for them.

The author of this book does not dispense medical advice or prescribe the use of any technique as a form of treatment for physical, emotional, or medical problems without the advice of a physician, either directly or indirectly. The intent of the author is only to offer information of a general nature to help you in your quest for emotional and spiritual well-being. In the event you use any of the information in this book for yourself, which is your constitutional right, the author and the publisher assume no responsibility for your actions.

Any people depicted in stock imagery provided by Thinkstock are models, and such images are being used for illustrative purposes only. Certain stock imagery © Thinkstock.

Print information available on the last page.

ISBN: 978-1-5043-5778-4 (sc)
ISBN: 978-1-5043-5779-1 (e)

Balboa Press rev. date: 07/05/2016

To the two luminous beings
I had the privilege of
bringing into this world.
May you continue to make
it a better place.

To my husband

My darling, you literally put your song in my heart every single day, you encourage me to write and to be creative. You are the best gentleman I will ever know and I am so immensely grateful to share this earthly journey with you in this, the winter of our life.

Contents

PART TWO

What this book is about

Higher Maintenance stems from the often-used expression "high maintenance", which refers to someone who demands a lot of frivolous things, attention and care.

I would say without malice that those of us living with a chronic illness are high maintenance (not out of a need for *more*) just to get by, taking care of a body that, at times, barely functions. Every day is a high maintenance day for us, and this soon becomes a heavy burden that affects all aspects of our existence.

This is why **Higher** Maintenance is so important! It is a way of life that involves a shift in perception and a new awareness of our selves and the world in which we live.

Higher Maintenance is the care of the heart and the soul so that we may find joy and peace in our day-to-day life.

It is my sincere wish that through my story and the few, very simple tools I share, you will discover your own unique ways to manage your dragon and your life.

Introduction

As far back as I can remember, I've enjoyed writing. I've had brilliant ideas over the years for book projects and titles. Or so it seemed at the time! I planned out a few outlines but never got around to finding a subject I would feel passionate about. It would have to be inspiring enough to compel me to write and rewrite for months until it conveyed what I really wanted to say. It would absolutely have to be the kind of book I myself would want to read.

It is common knowledge that a writer should write about what he or she knows. So I asked myself: What could I possibly know that could interest you?

One year followed another and I still wasn't writing a book. I did write a very good screenplay though... but that is quite another tale!

The story of my life is not that unusual; everyone's journey on Earth is a compelling story but I suppose not all of us feel the need to ponder the teachings that our life has offered, let alone put them on paper to share with fellow travelers on the road to wellness.

One thing I do know is what I learned from experiencing a traumatizing childhood: It leaves you ill equipped to handle the challenges of adolescence and adulthood.

I also know what I discovered through years of psychotherapy: It can take decades to undo the damage of early childhood abuse and neglect.

I read the books.
Did the work.
I accepted it.

As helpful and comforting as it was, I realized at one point that all the psychological and spiritual knowledge that I acquired over four decades did little to release me from the pain of my past. The yet unhealed wounds still hiding inside every cell of my body and every part of my soul overshadowed any chance of happiness coming my way. I had a knack for making the decision or taking the turn that led to sorrow and anguish, not because I lacked intelligence or intuition but because all my choices were based on fear.

I never, ever, allowed myself to let my guard down for a second. Fun was a luxury I rarely truly experienced because I didn't know how to let go. Something almost always spoiled my good time. That something often came in the form of migraines, dizziness, exhaustion, hypersensitivity or a feeling of panic. I overreacted to any and all unexpected events, even such trivial ones as a balloon popping or a knock at the door.

Life, as I saw it, was dangerous.

As much joy as my heart naturally exudes, I could never sustain and experience joy throughout one single day. If the term hyper-vigilance resonates for you, then we understand each other and I urge you to read on. I will tell you my story not because I am famous or so very different from anyone else, but because I hope it will show you that you too can move from a painful life to a joyful one.

With the help of wonderful online support groups, it is possible today to find well-informed advice and links on nutrition, supplements, medication and many other means to make life more comfortable. I will list my favourite resources at the end of the book. I will not go into detailed explanations about my particular chronic illness or about the latest research and discoveries. I simply want to focus on the *experience*, my own personal experience of life with "a dragon", as I call chronic illness. Let me guide you to explore how to enhance your quality of life and empower your self in the process. Each of us living with a chronic illness has expertise, a unique point of view. Mine is but one among countless other approaches that endeavour to make sense of things.

If you are new to a life that seems to be a shadow of your past life, I hope to bring you comfort, a deeper awareness of your place in this world, and support, along with a couple of useful tools. And if, like me, you are a veteran, then please take into account that perhaps I may not mention some of the things that you find important; in no way does that mean that I think they don't matter! I really don't want to paint an elaborate picture of what it's like to live with a dragon. Each dragon is different. What I want to do is convey that what we experience is real and it is very, very difficult to *embrace*.

Yet, embracing it is <u>the only way I know of, to find peace.</u> It is a bleak time in one's life when the dragon enters our space and, even worse, makes it long-term, if not permanent. I will paint this picture in broad strokes. I don't wish to dwell or invite sympathy that I don't need.

For those who live with or love a person struggling with chronic illness, it is likely that you will find here a better understanding of what they are going through. You will also be offered acknowledgement and recognition of what this does to you, to your life.

I have no magic recipe or gimmick. I simply believe that sharing the hard-earned knowledge that illness has allowed me to uncover can help change someone's life as it gradually transformed mine.

Because you have chosen to read it, you will very likely find something just for you within the pages of this book. A word, a sentence, a page or even a chapter will, I hope, ignite a spark of innocent hope that you can transform into joy! Why? Because

I believe that true joy from the heart radiates outward, and touches those seeking it. Now let's see how we shall learn to sustain joy while the dragon watches on...

PART ONE

Chapter 1

[ornamental flourish]

The day the Towers came down

I was 45 in the summer of 2001 and it was a time of great professional upheaval for me. After working as coordinator of a Volunteer Centre for nearly ten years, I was offered a position as director of a Food Bank, which provided services to 30 charitable organisations spread over a large rural territory.

Leaving my previous job meant that I would no longer enjoy the health insurance and benefits that a highly subsidised organisation could offer. As coordinator, I had run my own regional office, given training seminars and managed the activities of over 70 volunteers at any given time; I also sat on several community boards and panels whose missions were to improve the standard of living of the more vulnerable segment of the population.

My work targeted mostly the elderly and the physically handicapped. Over the years, I had created new programs like exercise groups, zoo-therapy visits and home library visits, while expanding existing programs like meals on wheels and community lunches. I was also organising fundraising activities, planning and designing brochures, getting free stuff from merchants, writing our own magazine and even writing, editing and publishing a book to raise funds for our activities. It was a great job! I totally loved it. The only fly in the ointment was my boss... the Centre's director. She was definitely competent but I had difficulty getting along with her, which I could handle largely due to the fact that our main office was 30 miles away. I didn't have to deal with her that much. She trusted me to run the regional office, a heated building that I had obtained from the town, rent-free. For a while, I was her shining protégée.

But as time went on, I think that my successes and popularity in the community became a problem for my boss. She began pulling me from panels, excluding me from meetings, shooting down every new idea I presented for projects, etc. I had less and less work to do and became bored. It is not in my nature to sit on my hands.

I went in as director of the food bank believing that a board of directors worked a certain way: the one I was used to, where board members let the director manage everyday activities. This group of nine elite members of the community however, thought that it was perfectly fine to have little meetings on the side and give orders to the director whenever an idea struck them. The concept of actually translating the organization's mission into structured actions was apparently foreign to them. A food bank gives food. Period. On any given day, I would get two or three phone calls from board members demanding that I run errands or make phone calls for them right away. All the while, my focus was on getting acquainted with the fundamentals of the organisation and with its daily activities. I also had to meet with our generous local suppliers and with the leaders of the organisations helped by our food bank. I decided to make a plan based on our mission; I prioritized and called a meeting of the board. To my surprise, my secretary showed up. I stated that she was not a member of the board and I was told that she took the minutes. OK... I wondered what the appointed secretary of the board's duties entailed, but I let that go for the time being.

The meeting went well and everyone agreed with my plan of action. Aaaand. Nothing changed. It was bedlam. I took work home and became so stressed out; it was ridiculous. The board members expected me to be everything to everyone 24/7 despite the fact that I had made my boundaries abundantly clear in my interview.

One morning, I woke up to find that I could not get out of bed. I was weak as a kitten and my throat was very sore. My husband helped me to the bathroom and I collapsed back into bed. He called the office and told my secretary I was sick with the flu.

My mind was floating in some sort of fog. I slept most of the time for a couple of days. When lying awake staring at the ceiling, I felt as though there wasn't enough air in the room. Although my airways felt unobstructed, breathing was becoming more difficult. I took every supplement I could think of to get over that flu and was back at work the following week. I felt awful. By mid-week, I asked my secretary to hold my calls, closed my office door and sat at my desk with my head in my hands. I prayed. Please give me a sign. What am I supposed to do here?

Looking at the piles of files and documents in need of my attention, I suddenly remembered that I had a meeting that morning with the president of the board and our biggest supporter who donated enough money yearly, to keep the food bank afloat. I had recently spoken to him to introduce myself and we had arranged to meet in my office at 9am this very day. It was now 9:35.

I ran out to my secretary and told her to call the president of the board to let him know that it was OK if he was running late picking up our sponsor and that we were keeping the coffee hot for them. I walked back to my desk wishing I had worn another outfit. A knock at my door was followed by my secretary opening it to inform me that the president of the board was at home with the gentleman in question and, that there was no need for me to come.

Thank you. Thank you. Thank you.

If ever there was a sign; that was it. I felt a mix of relief and anger. I was outraged that the president of the board would treat me this way, and thought he was an idiot. On the other hand, I now knew without a doubt that I didn't belong where I was at the moment.

I turned on my computer and wrote my resignation letter. I picked up the phone and called the only member of the board who had actually understood and supported my efforts. Christie was a local journalist who cared deeply for the people of our community. By 10:15, she sat in my office and read the letter, which I had to hand deliver to a board member to make it official. She was also outraged that the president had taken it upon himself to keep me from the important meeting I had arranged. Before long, Christie sat at my computer and wrote her own resignation from the board. We both cried because we knew that the food bank was in peril. How could the community and our sponsors continue to trust and support an organisation that had gone through five directors in three years? Yes, 5! After Christie left, I packed my stuff, informed my secretary of my decision and told her that my husband would come by to pick up the rest of my belongings. By the look on her face, she couldn't have cared less... She would get the run of the office again. Six months later, I learned that she was fired. Inappropriate actions concerning bookkeeping were rumoured in the community. The food bank was dissolved and its operations taken over by a large well-run organisation just west of its territory.

As I drove along the lovely country road taking me home on the day of my resignation, I only felt a huge sense of relief. I pushed aside the thought that I had previously left a virtually safe job for this nonsense and was now unemployed with a husband only working part-time. Like Scarlett, I would think about that tomorrow.

Two days later, I was struck down again, so violently ill that breathing was a chore and I thought I would die in my bed. My husband, Luc, was attentive and reassuring. After all, I had experienced a huge amount of stress in the last few months. I just needed a lot of rest. OK. REST. I focused on resting until two days later, at 11pm, I looked at Luc and said: 'Take me to the hospital, I am dying'. As soon as we arrived, I was rushed in through emergency, no waiting. My heart rate was all over the place. An oxygen mask was put on my face as we were informed that an ambulance was going to take me to a larger regional hospital to make sure I was not having a pulmonary embolism. My brain was swimming in a thick, peaceful sea of 'I don't care, this feels good, I can die, and it's OK'.

I was sent back from the regional hospital to my local hospital with good news: no embolism. After a battery of blood tests and physical exams, the doctors came to the conclusion that there was nothing visibly wrong with me aside from extreme exhaustion. They said I was probably experiencing a burnout and I was told to rest. As if I could do anything else.

Back home we went. I crawled into bed and let my mind swim in a thick and oddly blissful fogginess. I could hear the gentle stream outside my open window, my thoughts flowing away on it. I felt at peace for days. No reading, no TV, no music. My dog slept by my bed, patiently waiting for a decent walk. Luc brought soup, salad, toast, etc. And whatever he could put together, I gratefully ate. I eventually realised that I had not bathed or showered for at least a week. I couldn't stand it. I sat in the bathtub and for the first time, I cried out of weakness and helplessness. As I lifted my arms to shampoo my hair, my muscles felt like they had been set on fire. I lay back in the water and did my best to wash and then let the shower rinse me off, as I remained seated in the emptying tub.

Luc dried my hair and helped me back into the fresh sheets he had put on my bed. I was mortified that he had become my nurse and the one taking care of everything in the house. More importantly, my state of weakness was beginning to worry me. What was this? What if I had a mysterious illness and the doctors had missed it? I went to sleep that night with a vague sense of alarm and woke up the next morning with the first of several phone calls I would get that day.

It was my 46th birthday and I had not told any of my friends and family that I was feeling so poorly or that I had quit my job. Well wishes abounded and Luc did his best to make the day special with flowers, a homemade cake and a gift. Going out was out of the question but I did ask to sit outside for a while during that warm September afternoon. The wind on my cheeks and the smells of the mountains filled me with a gentle, hopeful energy that lifted my spirit. My body however, remained listless and unresponsive, exhaustion settling into my every cell.

The next morning, I managed to get up by myself and my weak, shaky legs took me to the living room couch as I held on to walls and furniture on the way. Luc brought me breakfast. It felt good to be out of bed. I turned on the TV to check what was happening in a world that seemed to have gone on without me. I glanced at the clock. It was around 8AM, September 11, 2001.

Images. Strange sounds. I remember no words. I watched replays of a plane hitting one of the two tallest towers of the World Trade Centre in New York City. I called out to Luc who came running in with a worried expression on his face as he turned to the TV screen. Along with the news anchors and the rest of America, we were in shock. As the people on TV were speculating as to the possible reasons for such a horrendous accident, the unthinkable happened. A second plane hit the other tower! Witnessed live by all on both sides of the TV screen, no words seemed appropriate to describe an event that would go down in history as the worst terrorist attack on American soil.

I don't remember how long I sat there, watching, numb. At one point, a reporter interviewed a police officer in the lobby of the first tower while we could plainly see behind them, the people that had thrown themselves out of the burning inferno and whose bodies hit the ground with a sickening thud. In a voice choked with emotion, the reporter eventually confirmed what this repetitive sound meant. I could not imagine the extent of desperation it took to jump out of a hundred+ story building to a certain death.

Then, there was a moment when everything came to a halt for me and for countless others across the planet. The first tower came down, crumbling like a house of cards and bellowing smoke and debris all across the city. Everyone in that building, workers with their children still in daycare, policemen and firemen were killed.

The world held their breath – as I'm sure you did – while other experts on TV were speculating as to why the tower had collapsed and what the odds were that the other one would too. It didn't take long for the answer to the second question to come. The second tower came down. Silence. The most seasoned news professionals, who had seen wars up close, had no words. I'm sure they began talking again at some point. But I was no longer hearing...

Cameras on the streets showed us apocalyptic scenes while deep inside of me, a knowing emerged. Sitting on my couch, hundreds of miles away from the towers vanishing over and over again before my eyes, I was struck by the symbolism of it: My life as I had known it, had crumbled around me.

I was an invalid.

To me, the towers represented the finality of my situation.

Could New York and America heal from this? Could I heal my own personal crisis? For now, all I felt was fear and numbness. I also wept at times for myself and for the people of New York City. I spent days witnessing and crying. It was so, so very sad seeing the thousands of pictures of missing loved ones posted on a makeshift board that seemed to go on forever along a street where there once stood two majestic pillars that seemed to touch the sky.

A week later, I sat in my doctor's office. Once I had told her the story of the sudden decline of my health, she sat back and said:

'I think you're experiencing depression'.

I rolled my eyes at her – it would turn out to be one of many such reactions from me to a doctor. – 'Gee, I am depressed? Of course I'm depressed! Who wouldn't be in my situation!'

She gave me a patient and understanding look and leaned forward. 'Look, as unlikely as it may seem to you, depression can cause all the symptoms you mentioned'. 'OK, I said, then why doesn't my therapist also think I have clinical depression?'

I had been seeing a therapist for the past six months. This was something I had done every so often throughout my adult life. I had studied psychology in university and had personally explored everything from Jungian psychoanalysis to a dozen other new approaches in the hope of healing the childhood wounds I still carried. I was currently working with a young woman who helped me make significant strides toward forgiveness, for others and for myself as well. Her method was very intuitive and my hypersensitivity was well suited for it. I needed to develop strong images and awaken emotionally disturbing memories so that I could express and release them. The amount of anger and sadness in me was still staggering after all those years!

So I left the doctor's office on that day, with a prescription for a mild antidepressant and instructions to return in three weeks. At home, I opened the pill bottle and held one tiny blue solution to my problem in my hand. I stared at it for some time, feeling as if I were in the Twilight Zone or the Matrix... Could this be me about to do this? Ignoring the voice inside that was screaming, 'Don't take the pill!' I swallowed it and went to lie down for a nap. I woke up a couple of hours later feeling no stranger than usual of late. Another pill before bed that night provided more kick. I woke up with a sensation that I had last experienced in my teens: I was floating like a fish in a lovely blue lagoon... totally stoned!

Luc made breakfast and I attempted to eat; I could not completely swallow. Drool came out of both sides of my mouth as I held my head up and tried to keep my eyes open. Something was very wrong.

Long story short, I ended up in the emergency room with a dangerously fast heart rate and six months later, after a couple more failed attempts with antidepressants to which I seemed to be allergic, my doctor ruled out clinical depression. A professional burnout was also taken off the table, seeing that I had been resting all these months without improving. In fact, my condition had worsened. I was extremely tired, headachy and sore everywhere. A new diagnosis was made: Fibromyalgia. I was given a prescription for pain and anti-inflammatory medications, and told to rest.

Thus began more than a decade of online research. I joined a support group and soon realised that these people with fibromyalgia were doing pretty well compared to me. It turned out that most of them were on low doses of antidepressants, which helped raise energy levels and lower pain. I was the youngest person in the group and felt totally out of place as I witnessed others dancing and enjoying themselves at organised suppers or festivities. They too, experienced very painful and difficult days, but my level of exhaustion was way more intense than anyone I spoke to.

Someone suggested that I might have Chronic Fatigue Syndrome, a vague term that the medical community did not acknowledge at the time. Since it had taken decades for Fibromyalgia to be considered somewhat seriously by doctors and since there was no cure anyway, it didn't make much difference to me. I just knew I didn't belong anywhere anymore and the remains of my previous normal life were disappearing.

A season for grieving

In more recent years, waking in the morning had been a time of hopeful enthusiasm, prayer and introspection until it became a reminder of pain, exhaustion, anxiety and the sorrow that my life had become. Getting out of bed was an Olympic event that required every ounce of strength I could muster not to scream in agony. The first few steps were the worst and eventually I was relieved to feel a lower level of pain that allowed me to get my day started. All my days were now more or less the same. I got my fruit, toast and tea and ate on the couch in front of the TV. Around 11, I somewhat made my bed and got somewhat dressed. By that time, I was wiped out so I rested. Luc made lunch when he wasn't working. I sat at the computer in the afternoon, searching for solutions but I couldn't sit up very long without experiencing severe back pain, which drained me of energy. Napped in mid-afternoon. Watched Oprah and General Hospital. Rested from that. Luc made most of our meals although I participated by doing what I could from a sitting position. Supper, a little TV again and early to bed.

I had always been an avid reader but that activity had become draining so I began to read in bed at night before going to sleep. Thankfully, I had no major sleep issues at the time and I managed to sleep through most nights.

I succeeded in making arrangements to collect unemployment insurance that would give me 75% of my income for 45 weeks; a little peace of mind for the moment. However, Luc lost his job and had no real desire to look for another one. A highly motivated – although undiscovered - artist, he had put together small local shows and was working on getting a government grant for another project while picking up odd jobs here and there. Our financial situation was getting tighter by the minute now. We lived in a rented mobile home up in the mountains, but even though we had no debt, we had no money to speak of.

As the weeks went by, our combined income was insufficient to meet our expenses. Luc did the grocery shopping and still came home with specialty bread, cheeses and wines as if nothing had changed. This made my level of stress increase tenfold, especially that he really was not looking for a job. We argued more and more. I pushed for him to find work while he progressively pulled away from me in every possible way. As a young adult, he had seen his mother whither away from cancer and I suspect he was protecting himself from another devastating loss. I'm guessing of course because our communications had dwindled down to the basic necessities, but my skin did have a grey tint and dark circles had developed under my eyes.

I had lost my work, my social and pre-Facebook era connections, my savings and most of the energy I needed to feel human. My cat and dog were my companions on an otherwise lonely journey. I did speak to my two closest friends now and then but the depth of my desperation and the pathetic life I was living embarrassed me, so as much as I sounded a tad mournful, I kept secret most of my pain or made light of it. I prepared my children, now young adults, for the likely possibility that I might be sick for a long period of time. Everyone was sympathetic but no one was there to see the extent of the hardships that marred my every waking moment. I kept from others, the pain, the fear and the anguish that weighed on my heart. I uttered nothing about the fact that I was losing everything that I believed made me, *me*!

As the months went by, I was in a sort of daze. I went through the motions and took care of myself as best I could, did a little housekeeping, some cooking and even managed to go out for some groceries once or twice as I held on to the shopping cart for dear life. The Holidays came around and it was customary that we spend Christmas Eve with my children and baby granddaughter at our place. That year, I asked the girls to pitch in and bring some of the food so I would have less cooking to do. I roasted the turkey and had set a lovely table the day before. I was glad to see the family together and we enjoyed opening gifts and sharing Holiday cheer but I found it all very exhausting. Still, I was doing much better than the previous summer and I didn't really look sick, so I made plans to go on with my life but at a slower pace.

Then they were more crashes or flare-ups that lasted weeks. During those dark times, I became listless and depressed. I was convinced I was dying. I didn't care. I wanted to die... I couldn't see through the heavy fog enveloping my brain, so I just lay there, waiting. Luc barely paid attention to me and seemed to resent having to let the dog out or feed the cat. I felt alone and desperately helpless. My children were in the city and my friends lived far away. My own mother didn't really believe I was sick and just thought I was lazy.

A part of me wanted to cry and cry but during a flare-up my brain was "wrapped in cotton balls" and I couldn't access my emotions properly. I just lay there and time seemed to have stopped although I could see the days go by through my window. I thought about God, my previous life, my children, people from my past, humanity. I tried to make sense of this human journey as I felt my soul yearning to leave this plane and soar out of this

16

broken body. I wasn't worried; I just observed what was happening to me and to the rest of the world; this world that really did go on without me! I felt that everyone in my life had forgotten about me just lying there day after day. As miserable as this experience was, I could sense something telling me that there was a reason for everything. Hope would make its presence known inside my heart. And so I lay there and waited for the storm to pass.

As one month followed another, I was more alone than ever. Spring came and brought a new breath of life to the mountain. I went on short walks with my dog, Jessie who loved frolicking and chasing the last few snowballs I'd throw. My arms ached and my legs shook, my heart raced as weakness brought me back to the couch where my cat would come and snuggle, purring with satisfaction. Those who believe that animals aren't that important to the sick would feel very differently if they lived in isolation and pain. The warmth and softness, the antics, all that animals bring to my life even today, is priceless.

Among my symptoms of CFS, for Chronic Fatigue Syndrome (Now widely known as Myalgic Encephalomyelitis, or ME/CFS), as it was called at the time, was an increasing sensitivity to just about everything from the texture of my clothes and the lighting, to sounds and smells, I always felt like there wasn't enough air in the room and sadly, I became allergic to my pets. Giving them up was out of the question, so I took antihistamines in low doses and washed my hands after I touched them. If I petted one of them and rubbed my eye, it would trigger intense itching, sneezing, congestion, etc. I had a minor wheeze with every breath I took but my pets were my family and I adapted.

Summer arrived and my unemployment cheques stopped coming. By a stroke of fate, Luc inherited a small amount of money from his father. It would be enough to get us through a few months anyway, and Luc kindly gave me a few thousand dollars to compensate for my dipping in my – now non-existent - savings to pay all the bills in the past nine months. That certainly took a load off my mind! But then I noticed that my cat, Spock, was becoming thinner by the day.

After a weeklong stay at the veterinary hospital, it was clear that he would not recover from kidney failure. I sat with him, held him and said good-bye and thanked him for the joy he had brought to my life. He was very weak but he purred as my tears fell upon his beautiful black coat. Spock was 10 years old when we buried him in the peaceful forest surrounding our home. If you have pets, you know that mourning a beloved animal hurts just as deeply as losing a human relationship or person. No, animals are not as important as people but they do matter very much to those who have shared their life with a cherished pet for many years.

Mourning the loss of my cat opened up an overwhelming amount of sadness that seemed to flow endlessly from my heart to my eyes, making my lids so swollen that I could barely see between them. I went from a state of shock to depression from one day to another. At times, I felt guilty for not having noticed Spock's declining health earlier; maybe I could have saved him? I held Jessie close to me and waited for the acceptance that would mark the end of this terrible grief.

In the meantime, I searched for tools, ways to manage my illness, this illness that had become my life! I reached out to Luc in a vain attempt to rekindle our marriage. I could see in his eyes that he was no longer invested in it and to be honest, he must have seen in mine that I had lost some respect for a man who would not do everything in his power to support his wife through illness and grief. I guess I was in denial where our relationship was concerned. I blamed the illness and figured that if I fixed that, we would leave a bad episode behind us and get close again. This was, after all, my second marriage and I was determined to make it work. We talked a lot about what we were feeling and did try to be understanding but 6 years after our wedding day, it was obvious that the 'spark' had dimmed a great deal. I couldn't dwell on that; I had to get to a better place health wise.

Chapter 2

Adapting to Change

Seeing my savings dwindle at an alarming rate, I decided to sign up for a yearlong weekend course in life coaching. I felt that, having been a psychosocial counsellor in previous years, I was well suited for this field of work. As a life coach, I could choose my own hours and put in as little or as much time as my health would allow. I was consuming quite a variety of supplements and ate reasonably well in an effort to strengthen my body.

Walking with my Jessie and breathing that wonderful mountain air made me feel stronger but still limited. I had a sense of optimism. This would pass; I would get better! That summer was luxuriously lazy and I daydreamed my days lying in the old swing by the brook near our house. I had fewer flare-ups during that period of total rest and it seemed that I had tamed the dragon.

Came September and I felt I was ready. I made the one-hour drive to the city every Friday evening for my weekend coaching classes. These lasted the whole two days and although I thoroughly enjoyed them, my body was aching. By lunchtime Saturday, I was wiped out. Fortunately, these classes were being held in one of the few large remaining working convents in the city. This wonderful place also rented rooms for short stays to people who needed quiet time. I had arranged to check-in the night before the beginning of class and could take a nap during the lunch break. The room was always perfect, the food was excellent but best of all, the whole package only cost $24 for the two days!

Quite a few of my classmates drove long distances and came back the next morning to resume our work sessions. I had had lots of rest and could handle another full day, albeit with some degree of difficulty. The nuns got to know me a bit and allowed me to stay longer after Sunday classes so I could lie down before making the hour drive back home. And so the year flew by and by June, I was a Certified Life Coach. Because I had many contacts in the health and welfare sector, it didn't take long to find clients among the many stressed out professionals who welcomed much needed support that didn't involve *therapy*. I also joined a businesswomen's organisation and got a few contracts among the many small businesses in my area.

I loved coaching and the money was pretty good... When I worked! I could barely manage 15 hours a week. On more than one occasion, I dragged myself to a session with a smile on my face and did my work all the while feeling my heart race wildly, pounding against my ribs. I would go home totally knackered and lie in bed wondering if I was kidding myself. Could I actually get better without any medical care aside from a bewildered family physician who had no clue what to do with me?

But then I would talk myself back to inner balance – I was a life coach after all – and gave myself permission to take all the time I needed to get better. If I had to cut my working hours, then so be it. And so it was.

By the summer of 2004, I was managing to keep working and to stay present in the businesswomen's organisation. I got voted on to the board of directors, which was a fun way to get extra visibility.

The heat waves that year were particularly intense. For people with ME/CFS, major changes in temperature are painfully difficult. Our inner temperature regulator is *offline* so we can be easily overheated or get the chills for no apparent reason. Before that time, I had only been vaguely aware that I had also become even more sensitive to a long list of irritants such as light, sounds, movement, etc.

A meeting was called for the board of directors on a muggy, sunny, hot and very windy day. The President of the group invited us to her house at the foot of a mountain I knew intimately, having spent most of my teenage years skiing and partying on its rolling mounds. We were sitting in her cool living room when someone suggested we sit outdoors to enjoy this wonderful day. I didn't object because of the enthusiasm with which this notion was received, although I knew this would make things more difficult for me. So, for an hour and a half, I sat there, wanting to die. The wind swept the sweat right off of me and made me shiver in misery. No one noticed except for the fact that I looked a little under the weather. Interestingly enough, all of these women were totally aware that I was living with a chronic illness and did nothing to try to make me more comfortable. Now you would think them heartless but the frustrating fact is that this illness, like many others, is *invisible*. I looked good, so all was OK...

The crash (or flare-up, or relapse, or PEM for Post Exertion Malaise), which followed this meeting, was catastrophic. During the weeks that followed, I basically lost my business and became very depressed. I lay in bed all day and watched the swaying of the trees through my window. I prayed and pleaded for help but could not find peace within myself, only sorrow. In more lucid times, I relived my last day in the outside world and took in the lesson that I must not be afraid to speak up when I feel that I am in a situation that makes me uncomfortable. It would be years before the lesson would sink in. We don't look sick so why would people believe us anyway, right? It is embarrassing to say that you have special needs and we don't want to be seen as prissy or demanding of attention. So we put up and shut up which is likely the reason we got sick in the first place, but I digress.

September would mark my 50th birthday and since I had almost always made arrangements for my modest birthday gatherings, I began to envision a celebration that would be a rite of passage: the beginning of my healing journey. I enlisted the help of my two children and of Luc. I wanted to invite my closest friends and my family. Together (twelve of us in all), we would sit outside for mealtime on our large balcony. My daughters would take care of the decorations and set up the table with Luc running errands and helping out. Guests were asked not to bring gifts, only wine and one dish to share. My wonderful daughters would coordinate all this. The one thing I would organise was a healing ritual.

With the help of some people I knew at my favourite health food store, I got in touch with a woman who was a Shaman of sorts. She performed ritual ceremonies where she summoned nature, helpful entities and the Creator to help with whatever was needed. She also included all persons present in the event that was to take place. We met and planned the ritual and the lady Shaman assured me that she would be there on the evening of my birthday to help me on my new journey.

The only person who refused to attend was my mother. This was no surprise to me but even after all these years, I still nurtured a hope that my mother would behave like one. I was disappointed once more. My lifelong feelings towards her were likely, after all, at the root of my illness and to this day, I believe we both would have benefited had she been present on that occasion.

It was a lovely and warm summer evening, the sky was cloudless and the stars came out; a million sparkling crystals on a jet black sky! After the festive meal, the Shaman arrived and prepared everyone for the ritual, explaining that their role was very important and that their state of mind and emotions were to be powerful allies in attracting healing entities. Men were the protectors, and were sent by the brook with their instructions. I was set down on a long garden chair and covered with two long hooded coats (because I was already shivering from the cool, early evening air). The men had prepared a fire before dinner and it was now gently glowing and crackling as the women took their places, quite naturally forming a circle around the fire at my feet.

The Shaman spoke as she summoned all the help that was in reach. Then she sat between two large crystal vases and began making melodious sounds punctuated by softly spoken incantations. I felt a powerful surge of energy, a glow that coursed through all of my being. Eyes closed, I focussed on my breath while the sounds filled me with a peace so enveloping that I felt as if I were flying.

Then the Shaman spoke briefly to the women before asking me to get up and walk with her across the road that led to our house. We faced north. She looked at me and asked me if I was ready to leave the past behind and make a definitive decision to *cross over* to my new life of healing, of health. She smiled as I made a commitment to move forward from now on, to put down the heavy load I had been carrying for decades. And so we walked across the road to my new life and rejoined the women. I lay down again and was covered with more blankets as I was still shivering. The women had been asked to think about one word that describes me best and were now invited to come forward one by one and tell me that word as they touched me and looked into my eyes. Although everyone smiled, most of us were deeply moved by this gesture no doubt meant to awaken my self-esteem and the emerging awareness that extreme self-care was called for.

I felt valued. Some of the words I heard surprised me. One of my daughters said: 'Courageous'. My other daughter could not come forward or utter a word, so moved was she. I understood that this was too much for her but I saw the love in her shimmering, dark eyes. No words needed. I really was valued.

I was cherished. I was admired. I mattered! Friends said things like: strong, loyal, joyful, and perseverant. Wow. I was swept up by a powerful, loving energy that I could feel flowing through my veins and all my muscles. My head felt light as a feather and my heart was overflowing with love, gratitude and faith.

The evening ended inside with cake and conversation. The ceremony had made an impression on everyone and it showed by the wonderful energy in the living room. I felt happy and very grateful to these people that mattered most to me, for taking part in this unusual birthday celebration!

I did experience a flare-up a few days later. I told myself it was because my body was healing. Was it?

Another winter found me in bed or on the couch. I took Jessie out for short walks almost every day because I felt I needed to move for fear of losing what little strength I had left. In spite of my resolve to heal, it was becoming clear to me that my life would never be the same. Gone was the old me. Gone was the life I could have had.

Could I accept a future I had not envisioned in my worst nightmare? Could I even manage to adapt, to find reasons to want to live this kind of life where there was no intimacy, no family, work or social life, no solution or cure in view?

As a rule, we humans dislike change. The changes brought on by a sudden illness that makes you feel like you are 90 when you are 46 years old, are astronomical. I lived in isolation and every movement I attempted caused so much pain and exhaustion that I failed to see the point of getting up in the morning. I was tormented by Luc's lack of interest and attitude, which was rapidly leading us to welfare. I decided that if I were going to live in poverty, I would have some control over my situation. I wanted out. Out of this life. Out of this world.

I cried day after day and all those tears finally stopped when I realised that there had to be an end to my marriage if there was to be a beginning to my healing journey.

Welcoming what is

It was on a cold, grey February day that Sandra, one of the two long-time friends I had left, drove more than 85 miles to come spend time with me. I lay on the couch and although I was extremely pleased and grateful to see her, I felt miserable and weak. We did a lot of talking, mostly about me, – sick people tend to be very self-centered; some might say with good reason! – and it was clear that I could not bear to live this way much longer. Sandra listened patiently, gently and kindly. She has a gift for sensing the meaning of non-verbal cues, every word and every breath. After the time it took for me to let out all the pain, anguish and deep sorrow that I was carrying, Sandra straightened-up, put down her cup of herbal tea, looked into my eyes and asked the question I had asked her and my coaching clients in their times of anxiety or despair: WHAT <u>exactly</u> do you want?

Smart lady!

This is a very difficult question to answer with precise clarity but it has an empowering and liberating effect when your heart opens up to reveal it. And you know your response is genuine when you have a strong emotional reaction. The answer was already springing into my consciousness: 'I want to be in my own quiet place with my dog and my fish', I immediately said as tears were pouring down my face.

As I was quite unable to do anything, my dear friend sprang into action. Two weeks later, she was back with a small van and with the help of Luc, filled it with 10% of my belongings, the essentials I would take with me to my new home; another 10% was furniture which would come via a small rental truck the next day. Sandra had found me a brand new, cute little 2½-basement bachelor in a beautiful house located in a quiet suburban neighbourhood not too far from where she lived. She had designed the space for the owner who, upon hearing my story, agreed to let me have the place at a reduced price. It was perfect! I could let Jessie outside through a window into the large back yard strewn with bushes, flowers and mature trees, plus a lovely brook that rippled alongside it. My Beta fish found a perfect spot on the window ledge of my kitchen sink where I could enjoy him.

I had with me, all that really mattered. It was a hardship to let go of most of what I had gathered over my lifetime: books, paintings, furniture, dishes, clothes, blankets, decorative pieces, etc. A whole wall of horseshow ribbons were put in the garbage, but I kept my first red ribbon and the first one I'd won a decade earlier on my beloved, now deceased, horse: Beaugeste. I entrusted my daughters with my photo albums and a few souvenirs from their childhood. I could take with me *only* the necessities of life and a few things that made my place feel like home; things I couldn't bear to part with. Leaving Luc was as easy as such things can be; the emotional bond between us had long been severed. I had no space in me to process the end of my marriage. The most difficult loss for me at the time was leaving my beloved mountains, the only place that had ever felt like home.

My daughters came to help me unpack and settle-in on the next day, when the furniture arrived. One of them drove my car to my new home since I was unable to drive more than 10 to 15 minutes at a time, off the highways. They were really wonderful about all this! And, the Creator always providing what we truly need: I now lived at the foot of a lovely mountain, one of a few in an otherwise mostly flat landscape. It was my rock, literally. My girls also provided me with a new computer that would turn out to be a lifesaver, a lifeline to the outside world and a means to both inform and entertain my self in the endless hours of solitude that awaited me.

I lay in bed that night, when everyone had gone, my body totally devastated by the stress and efforts of moving day. I looked up at the ceiling that would become very familiar and I thanked God. So many things to be grateful for! I felt both free and scared, but mostly free. This was a new beginning. This is where I would start healing. For the first time in a long time, I felt the presence of hope inside me.

The next morning, I woke up a lot more sore than usual but in much better spirits too! Jessie and I made a path through the many boxes still to be unpacked; I fed her and put her outside. I watched her explore the yard and I was glad to see that she seemed to approve. The necessities were unpacked, so I made myself toast and tea, sat in my recliner and turned on my TV; the rent for this little apartment included heat and cable too. From my new vantage point, I could see outdoors, and Jessie could let me know when she wanted to be let back in. Around 10am, sunrays lit the room; something we both enjoyed very much. I put down a plush little carpet where Jessie sunbathed whenever possible.

It took about ten days to get over the worst of the flare-up that followed the move. I expected it but not the intensity of it. I was so weak that I held on to the walls, boxes and furniture to go the very short distance to the bathroom and crawl back into bed.

Boring. Scary. Lonely. I stared at the ceiling. Prayed, cried, slept, waited for the storm to pass... for the dragon to go back into his cave. Sandra and the girls called to check up on me and offer help but talking was difficult, so I told them it would pass. Sandra brought some soup and a few other food items. I had given her a key so I wouldn't have to get up to answer the door. She wanted to help with unpacking or whatever else I needed and I assured her that for now, I really needed complete rest.

After a week being bedridden, I desperately wanted to wash. I filled my miniature bathtub, sat in the warm water and cried out of weakness and loneliness. I managed to rub baby powder through my hair, brush my teeth and put on a fresh pair of pyjamas before crashing into bed, totally wiped out. Every muscle was screaming from the strain I had put them through. I looked at the ceiling some more and a sense of relief washed over me.

One morning, I opened my window as usual and there was the unmistakable fragrance of spring in the air. I could hear birds and spy branches swaying in the sunshine. I breathed deeply, filling myself with a wave of energy that I needed so badly.

I gradually ventured outside with Jessie. We explored a neighbourhood that could be a postcard for the ideal suburbia. Perfect houses on perfect streets adorned with great trees. It was pleasant enough and very quiet. The occasional sign of human activity brought me near people who kept to themselves, so I had little contact with them except a nod or hello, which I prompted now and then. My sense of isolation was at an all time high but I tried to focus on the peace and quiet it afforded me. If I had any hope of recovering, I had to keep up morale. I found myself almost constantly pushing aside thoughts of self-pity and looking up at the sky.

The money Luc had given me was rapidly dwindling and the time had come to face the facts... I asked Sandra to drive me to the welfare office as soon as I was able to confront the emotionally difficult task of asking for financial support. How ironic that I had become one of *those* people that I used to help at the volunteer center not so long ago! I could now truly feel how humiliating it is to be in a situation where you have to say that you are so broke in every sense of the word that you cannot financially take care of yourself. I filled-in all the forms and was assured that I would receive a deposit within 10 days. I was given a number of flyers about food banks and other charities; I knew the drill. And, because I was claiming to be unable to work for health reasons, I was told that I would have to apply for a disability pension. In the meantime, welfare would continue to support me with the full amount for the disabled. I walked out with a sense of relief although I felt the stigma of being on welfare. I was now officially sick *and* poor.

Back home I went. During that first spring, I let loneliness envelop me like a cocoon while I managed to survive on my own.

I must state in all fairness that my daughters did drop by a couple of times with food and made lunch for us, cleaning up afterwards. Their visits wore me out but filled me with much joy. I was so sick but it didn't show at all. They listened to my complaints and were as understanding and encouraging as they could be, but clearly, they had no idea of what I was going through.

As I mentioned before, people with ME/CFS (Myalgic Encephalomyalitis/ Chronic Fatigue Syndrome), like many others with similar chronic illnesses, do not look sick. We get excited when people come to see us or when we get a chance to get out of the house; adrenaline kicks in and keeps us going for a while. But unlike healthy people, this extra adrenaline sends our system into a tailspin. The heart beats faster and everything else in our body is requiring a surplus of energy that we simply don't have access to. So we make more adrenaline, creating more stress on the body. We begin to feel very tired but the adrenaline makes up for the lack of energy, so we keep going. It may take 24 hours or more for our level of adrenaline to go back to normal. The feeling of exhaustion that follows is so extreme that it feels like impending death. Long after the visitors have left, thinking we look pretty good, they go on with their life while we feel the pain and heartache of another bout of complete, debilitating sickness.

I would learn in time, that each visit, each outing, every event, even a joyful one, had that one huge price tag. If the effort lasted too long, a flare-up would follow, lasting from four days to several weeks. This dragon was as big as a mountain and as powerful as an ocean. How on earth was I going to render it harmless, tame it, alone?

During one of my staring at the ceiling sessions – reading or watching TV was often too tiring -, it occurred to me that if I was to heal, I had to look at this illness as an ally and not an enemy. I had to welcome the dragon into my life because, perhaps, he was here to teach me something important. I suspected that this life was as lonely as it could be for a reason, a good reason, although it did not seem that way to me. So I decided to welcome my dragon! I listened to my body and became more aware of its limitations. Because I was living alone, I had no one to please but myself. If I didn't feel up to washing, so what? If the dishes piled up in the sink, who cared? I put myself first. Extreme self-care took on a whole new dimension.

By the time I had emptied the last box from the move, May had come around and the weather was much warmer. I still went on short walks with Jessie or sat on a bench by the brook. I watched buds burst forth with new leaves and blooms paint the yard with wonderful promises of flowers to arrive. The air had a smell so sweet that filled me with a sense of renewal and gratitude! I felt alive. I felt a part of this nature that surrounded me. I had seen brightness shine in my basement living room and now in our yard, as it made it's way to my heart, soothing the solitude and the pain, chasing away my fears. For now anyway.

I occasionally felt strong enough to go to the bank and get some groceries on my own. I cleaned my little apartment and kept it pretty. I managed to wash every second day and organised my schedule for other tasks like laundry. One task per day, 30 minutes to 1 hour of activity followed by 1 hour of bed rest. It was working. And then came another flare-up. I could not understand why. I found online communities and resources to get answers, but the dragon was quite unpredictable. Flare-ups could be kept at bay only some of the time.

One day, I spoke to the president of a support group for ME in the city. This lovely lady was also living with the dragon and for the first time, I could tell that someone really understood what I was going through. She gave me several useful references; one of them an endocrinologist at the City General Hospital who had taken a special interest in ME/CFS cases and even ran a research group at the nearby University Medical Centre. I was also referred to a lawyer who specialised in Fibromyalgia and ME/CFS disability cases, and took on legal aid clients.

I was so relieved and so grateful to know that I was not alone and that help was finally within my reach.

In the painfully crushing darkness that had tormented me for so long, I really did find a Light to guide and comfort me. It had always been there of course.

Chapter 3

In my own company

My daughters took turns driving me to several medical and legal appointments during the two years it would take to get my affairs in order. My ME/CFS specialist put me through a battery of tests to exclude the possibility of any other illness before concluding that I did in fact suffer from CFS. She also pointed out that some people – about 3% - spontaneously recovered from this strange and complicated illness, and it was still a mystery as to why they did. There was no cure and too little research to think that there would be one anytime soon. This was back in 2005.

I eventually got my disability pension and a hassle-free divorce.

During that time of uncertainty (is there any other kind, really?), I had to find ways of nurturing myself.

Once in a while, after doing groceries, I stopped at a nearby florist and bought myself one flower that I would enjoy for a whole week. On Saturday nights, I set a nice table, lit a candle and sat down with a glass of cheap wine as I dined, listening to my favourite standards. I didn't feel alone or sad. I felt nurtured. I could do this for me because I was worth it.

These were my first steps on the path of Higher Maintenance.

I thought about my kids, grandkids and friends and sent them kind thoughts and rejoiced in their success, trips and well being, as well as for their presence in my life in whatever capacity. On better days, I needed to express my youth and my joy, so I put on Rock'n Roll music and danced in my tiny kitchen, arms flailing, singing along in time with Brian Adams, Elton John, Rod Stewart and the Beatles. Music was an important part of my world. Sunday mornings were for classical music. Housekeeping or cooking (such as it was) were usually accompanied by my favourite artist: John Denver. His songs have soothed my heart and uplifted my spirit for as long as I can remember. During naps, I usually put on Enya or Tibetan sounds that helped me drift into relaxation. I couldn't bear silence in the beginning of this lonely journey; I found solace in the company of music.

But something else was missing among the other voids in my life, and that was work. I felt the need to be productive. An opportunity presented itself when a friend of a friend, who was working on a massive historical document, asked me if I would be willing to translate one of his projects. He could not afford to pay me but I was familiar with his work. It was based on the hidden spiritual aspects of historical events, and I knew the value of such knowledge for the seekers of this world. So, I began translating a manuscript about a subject that would give me a reason to believe I was contributing something to my fellow humans.

Another element now missing in my life was fun. A couple of years back, one of my daughters had given me a rather thick book entitled: *Harry Potter and the Order of the Phoenix*. I had mentioned seeing the first Harry Potter movie on video and liking it a lot. Living within a francophone culture, none of us knew at the time that this was a series of books. I so loved the book I got as a gift that I went out and bought paperback versions of the previous ones. Now seemed a good time to enter the world of J. K. Rowling's fabulous work. The time spent reading these wildly imaginative books brought me so much pleasure that I went through the series rather quickly in spite of my limitations. I was just so happy when I read them that they actually made me feel more energetic!

After re-reading *Order of the Phoenix*, which was the 5th book of the series, I went online to discover a whole new dimension of fandom. I learned that two more books were awaited with unimaginable

41

excitement by millions of people around the globe. Sophisticated websites were virtual meeting places for the exchange of ideas and theories between not just kids, but adults from all walks of life. I read essays and participated in discussions; it was brilliant! I also wrote two essays for my favourite online hangout.

If my translation work brought me deep spiritual insights and renewed my faith in my ability to contribute something to the world, Harry Potter strengthened my belief in magic. Those of you who have read and loved HP know what kind of magic I am referring to: The power of love over soul-crushing darkness; and you will understand if I say that I am a 'Gryffindor' through and through. In my experience, anyone living with an incurable illness is the essence of Courage. We may seem frail and easily broken at times, but we roar like lions and face that dragon every-single-day!

I now had many things to occupy my mind, my soul, and on a good day, time just flew and I felt okay. I was often frustrated when pain or exhaustion prevented me from writing or reading, and fortunately, I recorded some TV shows and movies I liked so that I could watch them later. I was a big fan of Grey's Anatomy and Boston Legal. I also still watched Oprah and General Hospital. Sandra was very busy working and was going through her own problems at home, so eventually, she didn't come around very often. For the most part, I was enjoying a solitary life. To my surprise, I found my own company rather pleasant! My fears of living alone were pretty much put to rest. The only exception was when a flare-up would rear its ugly head and bind me to my bed.

I never knew how long a flare-up would last or *if* it would ever end. During those endless hours, I was tormented by the fear of staying this sick, this helpless. I stared at the ceiling and cried, and prayed. I asked: Is this it? Is this my life from now on? Is the world just moving on without me, for good?

Inner strength

On better days, I kept myself occupied and entertained as much as my energy level would allow but the fact remained that I led a very isolated life. I thought about the future with no small amount of insecurity. I had seen neurologists, internists, psychologists, cardiologists, pain specialists and even a microbiologist but all my tests came up relatively normal. None of these doctors knew what was wrong with me; let alone how to help me. My ME\CFS doctor also sent me for scans, ultrasounds and other more sophisticated tests. Besides slightly elevated cholesterol levels and low white blood cell count, it seemed that my heartbeat was irregular but nothing to worry about.

I suppose there is some kind of relief in knowing that you don't have cancer or multiple sclerosis but there is also a sense that *something* is really wrong and the mysterious nature of that something is scary. I was 52 years old and disabled with no clue as to why. Sometime during my first year living alone, I began to develop intense, very disturbing and painful tingling sensations with needles and pins in my hands and mouth. My skin became extremely sensitive to the point that my clothes were causing me pain. I was also becoming increasingly sensitive to light. Although he had no idea what this was about, my neurologist prescribed Gabapentin.

I began taking this drug that incapacitated me even more severely and did little to ease my pain. I was already taking a low dose of Xanax to help me fall asleep at night. After weeks of this hell I was going through, my neurologist suggested I try Lyrica, a drug in the same family as Gabapentin but recently FDA approved for Fybromyalgia pain. This time, I took the lowest possible dosage and increased very slowly until I felt some relief.

Experience tells us that ME patients are hyper-reactive to all drugs. Most doctors are clueless about this; and so began my understanding that I would have to educate medical professionals in the future. I found a level of Lyrica that did turn down the pain volume (my clothes or a strand of hair in my face no longer 'cut' into me) while allowing me to be fairly functional, but the tingling in my hands still bothered me. I then found a family doctor (GP) near my new home, which in parts of our country is nothing short of a miracle. I handed her a file and sat at her desk, well prepared for receiving the only health care I could expect. I told her about my journey in the previous year and gave her sheets of test results. I said that I needed her expertise and that she needed mine: we had to work together if she was to help me in any way. She agreed to a partnership in the management of my healthcare. She took time to read the material I would give her and learned a bit about ME. I suggested the dosages of my medications and she went along with the knowledge of my illness, knowledge that she was aware I possessed.

One day, some weeks prior to seeing this new family physician for the first time, I got so fed up with the tingling sensations in my hands that I took a Xanax in the middle of the day just to calm down. The tingling had gone away. I went back to the Pain Centre. When the team of pain specialists heard about the Xanax (a common anti-anxiety medication) helping with the tingling sensations, they told me that in their expert opinion, my health problems were caused by anxiety. I was amazed that after at least eight years of medical training, these so-called specialists dismissed me and told me to see a shrink, in spite of the fact that they had been given evaluation reports from two different psychiatrists stating that my mental health was sound. It's enough to drive someone... nuts.

My new family doctor however, prescribed Xanax and told me to take up to 4mg throughout the day if needed. To this day, I never exceeded 3.5mg per day (including my nightly 1mg) in spite of the fact that this drug causes resistance and addiction. Not so for me. I am dependant on it to be sure, but after eight years, along with 250mg of Lyrica a day, Xanax keeps the tingling sensations under control most of the time. As for the fibro pain, I managed it – still do - with acetaminophen or codeine on really bad days. I also still use heat and relaxation, walk a little and do a few yoga-inspired stretches in the morning. I also take a myriad of supplements mostly to increase my energy level and balance my immune responses.

I was very relieved to have found a doctor that listened and understood that her role – for lack of knowledge as to how to treat ME - was to help keep me be as comfortable and functional as possible. The Xanax/Lyrica mix was working for me but there was a price to pay. I became more tired, clumsier and more forgetful. I had an increasingly tough time with word retrieval. These symptoms are largely due to the illness of course, but the medications increased their intensity. Another side effect was that they made me feel a little more detached from emotion – turning down the volume, so to speak -, which would turn out to play in my favour.

Flare-ups, i.e. crashes, still came and threw my hard earned and still fragile peace of mind right out the window. I lay in bed for endless days, wondering if this was it; if this time I would not get "better". I was only too aware that a large number of people with ME/CFS remain in this state of flare-up and never recover. I managed to get Jessie out the window to the yard a few times a day. I always had ready-made meals in the freezer and raw veggies and fruits on hand. Eating, letting the dog out and going to the bathroom were the only things I was barely able to do during those lonely and miserable times. Jessie would get restless after a while, but she seemed to know I was too ill to take her for walks, so she mostly slept. I loved to watch her sleep peacefully and was grateful for another beating heart near me. Sweet, sweet Jessie! Tears ran down my face as I thought of her energy and enthusiasm and of how she made my life bearable.

Washing was still a major issue during flare-ups. I would sometimes stand at the bathroom sink and look at the dishevelled woman in the mirror without any recognition of the pretty lady I used to see there. Dark circles had taken permanent residence under the eyes that looked back at me with so much sadness. I looked my age I suppose, (I have always appeared to be younger than my actual age) but I felt 90 years old; a weak and battered one with shaky legs and arms. I would hold on to the sink, sweating from the effort, and reach for my hairbrush. Holding up my arms set my muscles on fire as I tidied up my hair but I did it anyway. On other days, I would manage to brush my teeth thinking how ironic it is that we take such a little task for granted when we are healthy.

When a flare-up lasted more than a week, I had to wash. My scalp was itchy and, although I didn't care all that much during these times, I knew I smelled. So, I would fill up my miniature bathtub and sit in the warm water and cry. 'God', I prayed, 'please, please help me'! I couldn't lie in the tub, so I put up my legs on the wall facing me and sat back so my hair would be in the water. Looking at the ceiling, I sobbed. Where had my life gone? How ridiculous was this? Unable to shower and having to lie in a mini tub, gathering the strength to wash myself. With my heart beating alarmingly fast and hard against my ribs, I eventually crawled back into bed somewhat cleaner and totally spent. When people say they are tired, they only have a minuscule notion of tiredness. For people like me, tired is what I feel on a really good day. When I say that I was spent, I mean that even breathing was a huge effort.

After washing, it would be several hours before I could get up again. Day after day, I spent all these hours in bed, mostly awake, thinking, praying, crying, feeling sorry for myself, and feeling guilty for feeling sorry for myself. I could listen to relaxing music for a while and think of nice memories and images. But I missed my friends, my family, and the time when I could *be* there for them... Sadness would overwhelm me and the crying would start again.

After a flare-up, I slowly began to feel alive again, life seemed full of promise and I felt hopeful that I could get better. It would take approximately two weeks to get back to my new 'normal' energy level, which, at the time was 4.6 on my own scale of 10. Flare-ups dipped to a 2/2.5. A 1 is very close to total system failure. (There are more detailed scales out there, but this is what I began with to better make sense of my energy situation.)

Having gotten back on my feet, so to speak, I started walking Jessie, much to her delight. I would look down, amazed that my legs were holding me up because I still felt so weak.

One day, I decided that it was time for me to see a massage therapist as I had done in past, pre-illness years. The expense was now enormous for me but I knew my health would improve with treatments geared to increase my energy levels and ease some of the pain I was dealing with on a daily basis.

I picked up some leaflets at the health food store and there were many to sort through. I tossed most of them aside because it had become easy for me to spot the real healers from the would-be miracle workers. This is when Julie entered my life, or rather, when I entered her home for my first visit with her. She welcomed me in a small treatment room that felt calm and nurturing, just like Julie herself. I sat and looked around at the soft, blue and purple hues, the many crystals and few images that inspired serenity and wellness. Julie explained how she worked. I described my condition in more detail so that she would take into consideration that I would literally break if given a rigorous massage or one that was intended to be "in depth". I sensed that she understood completely. She was a combination of strength and vulnerability and I could tell she was on her own healing journey of sorts. As I lay on the massage table, enveloped in warmth, soothing music and pleasant odours, she closed her eyes and as she breathed deeply, I felt connected to the force that came through her.

I drove the short distance home after my massage and went to bed as soon as possible. My legs felt like rubber. I slept till suppertime, Jessie's suppertime. I was achy but wonderfully relaxed. I hurt badly for the next few days but I had a sense that something was shifting in my body and energy was circulating more freely.

My sessions with Julie would be few, as I could not afford to continue. During this short period of time, a friendship was growing between us. She offered me tea after our sessions and her cats would settle on me, reminding me of the joy of hearing a soft purr and gazing into the bottomless pools of a magnificent, hypnotic feline stare. Julie and I talked about our life, our spirituality and our journey on the road to enlightenment. One day, she offered me a chance to be one of her subjects for the final stage of a course she had been taking. I'd get six free treatments! The fact that they were centered on releasing old, unresolved wounds from every cell in the body was very appealing to me. No massage was involved. Her hands hovered over me as she focussed on *being* a channel for the invisible aid that was available to us and who asked nothing better than to be of help. I was given visualisation homework to do.

Over time, Julie and I went on short outings, enjoying the sweetness of summer. We'd have lunch on terraces by the river or shop in a used bookstore where I completed my Jane Austen collection and even found the entire Lord of the Rings trilogy, much to my delight. We'd sometimes lunch while sitting on the grassy ground in front of the town church or enjoyed ice cream cones in a nearby café.

Julie, it would turn out, would become a dear friend. She understood my condition and never hesitated to drive if we went somewhere. We'd invite each other for supper on some Saturday nights since we were both divorced, and opened a bottle of wine. Every outing cost me days of recuperation but they made me feel almost normal again.

More than once, during a healing session with Julie, I heard voices; very short and distinct messages. I felt the Light that was coursing through me and sometimes saw the shimmering outlines of powerful aids in the room with us. It is very difficult to describe to anyone who has not experienced such events, but I can only say that it felt like my heart was sailing. Yes. Heart sailing! There was this space where I didn't have to be strong; I just had to let go. I was so very tired of being strong that these times of visualisation became part of my new extreme self-care regimen. I began to take my eye off the dragon for short periods of time and focused on my faith, on the help that was available to me at any moment of the day. I was NOT alone. I had never been alone. No need to be strong. Just let go...

***********In loving memory of my dear friend********
Julie
*who passed away shortly before
the publication of this book.
A beautiful soul on a journey to a beautiful place.
Merci ma belle Julie !*
****

Chapter 4

Test of faith

Some people think that letting go means giving up. It actually means something quite different: It means Trust. Trust in Life. For me Life is God. That is my own belief but whatever yours may be, the essential core of letting go is to trust in Life, in that flow of energy that makes up the universe, which we are a part of. We are tiny oceans of energy, sparkling drops in the vast cosmic ocean that is Life!

I was in a good place for a while, sorting out my new attitude toward my condition. I did feel a small increase in my energy levels and that fuelled my belief that I was on the road to recovery.

And then it all happened.

First, my friend Sandra, who had moved me to my new home, made herself more and more scarce. I would telephone her, only to get her voice mail. She eventually stopped returning my calls altogether. I dismissed this because I knew that her career was keeping her extremely busy. She was also now going through a very unpleasant divorce from a controlling man. I had felt her anxiety when she came over for brief visits, but I didn't realise that something was seriously wrong with her. After all, she had always been so successful in everything she did and I admired her strength and positive outlook on life.

In a few short months, Sandra completely disappeared from my world and I had no way of getting in touch with her. I didn't even know her address, – she had recently moved - only her email and cell phone number. I figured she needed space. After all, sick people can be quite a bit of a chore and she had done a lot for me. One day, she showed up at my door with a box containing letters and papers. She read me a long letter from her soon to be ex-husband. It was cruel and vindictive. Sandra seemed terrified of him. 'I'll let him have anything but my child', she said. She'd let him keep the house and asked for nothing in return. I listened and gave her some comfort and advice along with a glass of wine. She left feeling better. We hugged. I didn't hear from her for almost two months after that visit. She called to say she was now on anti-depressants and seeing a psychiatrist 4 times a week. I was shocked to hear that she was going through a major depression, a total breakdown. Brené Brown calls it a "spiritual awakening". I totally agree, but I didn't realise that then.

At the time, for all intents and purposes, I had lost my friend. She asked me to understand and to be patient. She could be a friend to no one for an indefinite period. She would contact me when she got better. That would turn out to be two years later. I was devastated for her and for myself. I was now without the support I had counted on in moving so far away from my kids and from the place I knew as home. I thanked God that Julie was in my life. But Julie had not signed on to help take care of my needs and I did not ask. She was a friend I could confide in and that in it self, was a comfort.

Then came the second event that shook my life in the same period of time. My daughter, Sarah, had just spent the summer in South Africa following the end of a serious relationship, when I noticed she sounded very sad every time I spoke to her on the phone. She said she was tired all the time and didn't feel like doing anything.

Occasionally, I would spend a weekend at her house. But one day, Sarah seemed so overwhelmed over the phone that I asked if I could come spend a week with her. My other daughter, Amy, picked me up and on the drive there, we talked about her sister. She was very worried about her. Neither of us had ever seen Sarah in such a state of complete despair.

My heart sank when I entered the house. There were heaps of clothes on the floor, dirty dishes in the sink and no free space on the counters. The hardest thing of all to take in was the look on my beloved child's face: Her beautiful eyes were filled with sadness so profound that she had no more tears. She was curled up on the couch in her pyjamas, covered in a blanket and surrounded by used tissues and half emptied glasses and cups. She sat there all day, sleeping or looking out the window.

We had many talks during that taxing week. It was unmistakably clear to me that she too, was in a deep depression. I urged her to go see her father's private doctor (for a prompt appointment) and I helped around the house as best as I could.

A week after I returned home utterly exhausted, I got a call from Amy frantically telling me that something was really, really wrong. Apparently her sister had been prescribed anti-depressants and was having what looked like a manic reaction. She was seemingly out of control.

Amy came to pick me up and I set up camp in her apartment for a couple of weeks. She told me that a few days earlier, my children's father had attempted to reason with Sarah and the conversation had escalated until all hell broke loose. Sarah was now certain that we were conspiring against her. She was sending nasty emails and leaving hostile messages on our voice mail. I had become the enemy and could no longer reach her. The unthinkable had happened: both my closest friend *and* my daughter were in psychosis. I had to be strong for Amy who was having a hard time wrapping her head around the fact that her sister was no longer her friend.

For days, I researched online for every possible resource that could offer support. My children's father had a private detective follow Sarah to make sure she was safe and to build a case for legally getting her to undergo further evaluation and better treatment. We even had a family meeting over the options open to us. Being an adult, Sarah was free to do as she wished. And she did! In the span of three weeks, she maxed out her credit cards and the one her father had given her for emergencies. She bought furniture and everything imaginable that struck her fancy.

She eventually agreed to have a second psychiatric evaluation where the family was allowed to express their concerns. Their father did not have the time to show up, so, Amy and I presented evidence to the psychiatrist.

We clearly demonstrated that Sarah was not herself and that her capacity to function responsibly was seemingly impaired. Sarah sat there with a smug look on her face and listened quietly. The doctor thanked us and asked us to exit his office. We were very shaken by the whole experience and sat in the hall to gather our wits. We felt that we had betrayed Sarah and it was a small consolation that it was for her best interest, as far as we could tell.

Sarah walked out of the office no more than fifteen minutes later, her hands wrapped around the arm of a strange man she had recently hooked up with and who did not inspire confidence in Amy or in me. She laughed as she strutted past us and straight out the clinic door. I was outraged! All this work to get her a new evaluation and appropriate treatment had amounted to a mere chat? I demanded to see the doctor who very plainly told me that since Sarah was an adult, he was under no obligation to discus her case with us. Nevertheless, he added that in his opinion, she was just fine. Amy and I felt totally defeated. We could do nothing but watch a loved one in danger of spiralling even further out of control.

Thankfully, it would be over in a matter of a few more weeks. After throwing away her anti-depressants, Sarah eventually regained her grip on reality only to realize that she had to rebuild her world practically from scratch.

Meanwhile, I had returned home completely drained of energy. I became very weak and slipped into another soul-crushing flare-up that lasted weeks. I felt so alone. I wanted to be a mother for my children and could not be. That was the hardest of all. Both my girls were in pain and I was lying in a bed staring at the ceiling. I slept and cried. I took care of Jessie, fed the fish and managed to go to the bathroom and throw a ready-made meal in the microwave or eat some fruit and granola bars.

The cycle of sleeping, crying, praying and feeling sorry for myself went on until one day, I felt a powerful surge of anger rise inside of me. I looked at the inspiring spiritual images on my wall and a scratchy voice rose out of my throat: 'God', I cried, 'what do YOU want from me? You want my blood? Take it! You want my bones? Take them! Take everything! You've already taken my home, my work, my family, my friends, every cent I had! Take it aaaall!!' I wailed in anger and spite. For what seemed like hours I lay there, furious at God. What was the point of being a decent person, I wondered; what was the point of living? I had no life. I did not want this life. I was in agonising pain and I wanted it all to go away.

I wanted out.

I stared at the full container of Xanax on my night table. It would be so easy... I took a deep breath as I imagined how wonderful it would be to fall asleep and never wake up. The thought calmed me down for a while. I remembered reading that the first cause of death in people with ME\CFS is suicide. I also recalled saying in the past that I would *never* do such a thing. Well, now I got it. I understood. I suddenly truly understood why people take their own life. It is a fact that I now know for sure: Only if you have been in so deep a despair can you understand what it feels like to want to die. It is a dark and Godless place.

God is Light and Light is Life. Only darkness remains when you feel yourself sinking into the deepest, deadliest despair.

I was filled with a strange sort of relief as my sorrow was replaced by the powerful energy of anger. My heart was pounding and my fists were clenched. For the first time in weeks, I felt alive...

I fell asleep.

When I woke up a few hours later, Jessie was asking for her supper. I gathered up the strength to feed her and let her out. As I watched her run around the yard in playful bounds, I found myself smiling. It had just occurred to me that it was a lovely, sunny day, I pushed the window wide open and breathed in wonderful, new, fresh air. How good it felt to fill my lungs with the sweet smell of life! Tears of peaceful gratitude ran down my cheeks.

Once I had climbed back in bed, I stared at my inspiring images on the wall. God was there. God filled me with His grace in spite of my anger at Him. This time, I wept with joy. And with sorrow. But mostly with joy. I had come to realise that wanting to die is simply a desperate need for the pain to stop. At no point in my life have I ever doubted God. For some, faith is merely wishful thinking; for others, it is imaginary fantasies of an old Sage sitting on his throne and deciding what happens to whom. But for many, many of us, it is an intimate experience, a "knowing" that can only be understood by those who have felt its power. As is the case with despair, those who have been there understand faith. This reminds me of the film *Contact*, a perfect example of this. In the movie, the character portrayed by Jodie Foster is a scientist and an atheist. She believes only in what she can see, measure, and calculate. But when she experiences something extraordinary that she is asked to prove, she can't. We see that moment when she gets it: Faith is something that you experience, that moves you to the core of your being, and *that* is why you believe.

That evening, as the sun was setting on yet another day of misery, I made my peace with God. I asked for His forgiveness and chose to continue believing that His Justice may not be visible to us on Earth, but it is perfection. If I was to experience this illness, it had to be for a reason; the dragon was not going to weaken my faith. In fact, since then, my faith has only been made stronger with every passing day.

I gradually regained some strength and walked outside with Jessie. I was amazed at her boundless energy and the irony did not escape me: She had so much of what I lacked... I rejoiced in the thrill that running around the yard at full speed gave her. Sitting on the little bench by the brook, I looked up at the sun peering through the tall trees and marvelled at the splendour of nature as I hummed a song.

One day, I stood up near the brook and wrapped my arms around a tree, smelled it's wonderful earthy fragrance and leaned my cheek against it. I could hear the life within it and I hugged it. Yes, I confess; I am a tree hugger. Hey, I get energy wherever I can! Trees, especially birches, pine and spruce trees have always given me strength just by looking at them or touching a leaf or smelling needles. And now, I had found a way to commune with them by wrapping my whole soul in their mightiness. I felt life coursing through my body and my heart. And that is a very good thing.

Asking for help

One of the many difficult issues that surface with chronic illness is finding yourself in a position where you must, sooner or later, ask for help. Naturally, the first responders in such a case are spouses or partners, live-in family members, other close relatives and very close friends. As is true for too many of us, the stress that my condition brought to my marriage ate away at our relationship and it did not survive.

I cannot over emphasize how illness affects the people with whom we share our life. It is not only our world that is turned upside down; it is also theirs. From a partnership of relatively equal proportions, one of you becomes more and more a giver, not by choice but by necessity. For some couples and families it is an opportunity for circling the wagons, so to speak, and for becoming closer by facing this challenge together. Sadly, more often than not, the burden of caring for someone in loss of his or her autonomy – at so many levels – is just too much to handle. I have sincere empathy for those who make the difficult decision of withdrawing from a life they did not choose.

To those who stay because their love is stronger than the fear of living *differently*, I say: You are heroes!

To the spouses that now cook, clean, make their sick loved one smile; to the partners that help change our clothes or rub our back, although after a long

65

days' work outside the home, they could really use a back rub; to the children of mothers who can no longer entertain them (or play with them if they are little); to young adult children who must become caretakers, putting aside their own weariness and drive long distances or do the parents' groceries for them when they, themselves, barely have the time to do their own; to the friends who 'stay' – and there are very few who do – when it is they who must do the driving and bring a meal when they visit; and to the same friends who allow you to vent, to talk about your pain and listen with an open heart, take you out to lunch or a movie; to strangers who smile and say 'hello' when you are out for a short walk, strangers who have no idea that they may be the only human contact you'll have all week; to neighbours who show that they care by doing little gestures like bringing you their latest sample of homemade jam in a cute little jar: To each and everyone of you, we who are ill say ***thank you*** with every breath we take. Thank you for doing the best you can even if our needs seem bottomless.

Thank you is not nearly enough, I know. When I stop and think about it, I realise that I am often left with more needs after someone has helped me and that it leaves them with a sense of frustration or perhaps guilt. I have had the impression that my children have felt betrayed by my being ill. I should be the one helping them... They must know that at some level even if they assure me that it's OK. It's not.

However grateful we may be, and we are, make no mistake; the fact is that when you are feeling so poorly, so ill, *everything* is about you. That is the bottom line. We become selfish just to survive and we are riddled with guilt for being a burden to those we love.

That is one reason I chose to live alone and ask as little as possible from my small network of people willing to help. I asked for help only for absolute necessities. I kept my misery to myself, for the most part...

So it was that two years after leaving to live on my own, I had exhausted my financial resources and in March 2007, I called a charitable organisation and signed up with a local food bank. I still had my small 12-year-old car and could make the short drive to the nearest church basement for the weekly pick-up. Another ironic twist to my life: I had gone from director of a food bank to one of the poor, waiting in line for free food. The first time I went, I looked around and observed the volunteers at work. I knew the system very well. It was like going back in time, only from a very different perspective.

My ego was protesting mightily. I felt extremely humiliated. After a few weeks, I became ashamed to admit to myself that all the time I had been working as volunteer services coordinator and later as director of the food bank, part of me had been judging the healthy-looking recipients of food, welfare and other donations. After all, a lot of them seemed quite able to work; I had wondered what they were doing on welfare or in a food bank.

This food bank provided an area where you could sit down after getting a number to wait your turn. I watched little kids run around as the mothers chatted with each other. Some older people waited quietly. There were young men staring blankly into space, tapping a foot or wringing their hands. Looking around me, I found no one with whom I could identify: I was NOT like these people. But yet there I was, openly showing the level of my neediness.

As the weeks went by, I became more comfortable and did find some things in common with the others who, like me, were asking for help to make ends meet. Smiles and greetings were exchanged. I would go home with several bags of fruit and veggies, soymilk and puddings, cheese, bread and even some baked dessert. Yes, the food was surplus from local grocery stores, but it was still perfectly good food. I was so grateful. What bounty!

There was also a place where I could go every six weeks to receive donations of non-perishable goods and even some frozen meat. And when Christmas came around, I was invited to sign up for a special treat, courtesy of local businesses. In an empty arena, a shopping area was set up so that we could use a cart and choose from a great variety of products such as shampoo, lotions, basic clothing like socks, slippers, mittens and hats. There were also canned food and other non-perishable goods. We were accompanied by a volunteer who would make sure that we took the amount of merchandise matching the number of people in each household. Even though I was alone, I left with so many wonderful gifts! I was even given an envelope with a $25 card for groceries at the local supermarket.

I now profoundly understood how giving to charitable organisations, whether it is time, goods or money, makes a huge difference for people who are struggling. I saw the look on some recipients' faces and the expression in their eyes was often one of graceful gratitude. Yes, there will always be those who lazily take for granted the free stuff they receive, but they are few. It is only when I saw for myself, what poverty looks and feels like, that I felt it was OK to be one of *them*; one of the needy. We don't always know why folks get into such a place in their journey and until we do, it is best, I believe, to give them a compassionate thought.

I remember waiting for my weekly food, watching the younger kids play. They wore tattered clothes that were once expensive and fashionable but they didn't care; they had the best of time running around together. I can still hear their sweet laughter that made me smile at the mothers who attempted to keep them quiet so as not to bother the other people waiting their turn. Let them laugh, I thought, they are real and without judgement of others or of themselves. Those children made it all bearable. They made it OK to be there and get free food. They didn't know they were poor and for that reason, they were NOT. And nor were the rest of us.

I would go back home totally spent from my outings at the food bank. As I lay in bed afterwards, once I had put away the food, I would reflect on poverty: It is a state of mind, that's all. It is a label that we use to classify a portion of our society that is mostly invisible. Just like people with invisible illness, they bear a load of huge proportions that most people can't even begin to imagine.

I became kinder after my experiences at the food bank; kinder to myself and to everyone I would meet ever since. I let go of my self-imposed shame and congratulated myself on having the courage to ask for help. It is, I feel, an act of respect and kindness toward those who need to *give* help. How wonderful that they experience the joy of giving thanks to those who receive much needed help! There is something sublime in this exchange; having been on both sides of it, I can now allow myself to give freely and to receive gracefully.

Learning to overcome pride in order to ask for help is one of the numerous and precious gifts that illness has brought into my life.

Chapter 5

The voice of aloneness

I remember the many times I was left alone as a young child. As much as those times had frightened me in the beginning, I eventually felt that being alone was also a safe state of being. No one to abuse me or yell at me, no one arguing in another room to the point that I was afraid to show my face. As an only child, aloneness was a familiar place for me and therefore, became comfortable.

Since adolescence, I've had many relationships of the romantic kind and by the time I was well into my forty's, I had not totally gotten over my first love – does anyone, really? – Anyway, I always had a man in my life. My friends had pointed out that I was dependant on affection and attention. Perhaps they were right.

Illness brought me face to face with solitude; a long-time solitude that I would not have chosen otherwise. I lived on my own for five years of aloneness that would change my life. Yes, another gift from the dragon.

When I first found myself truly by myself, I was in shock but as the months went by, I began to feel that same safe state of being I had known as a child. There is something to be said for doing what you want to do – or are capable of doing – when you want to do it. It is a luxurious sensation to forget the clock and just let the day unfold. When I was not in a flare-up, I would get up pretty much at the same time each morning and I did have my routine of taking care of Jessie, having breakfast in front of the TV morning shows and enjoying a second cup of decaf at the computer. Resting time followed each activity after that. Eventually, I had made my bed, washed up and changed into my sweats – or any really soft and comfy clothing – by lunchtime.

To this day, I am always amazed when I hear comments such as: 'I'm tired too, but I have to go to work anyway even though my back hurts; you have to push through and stop being so lazy'. Or: 'But you don't look sick; I think you are obsessed with vitamins and pills; go out and get some exercise!' Or: 'Stop thinking and talking about your illness; if you focussed on other things, you'd get better'. And my personal favourite: 'Boy, I wish I could sit around all day and watch soaps!' In spite of the very large amount of information out there on the net today, the vast majority of people, including most health professionals, have no idea of the soul-crushing pain that those of us with chronic illness must endure. But I digress.

Afternoons were devoted to naptime; a couple of hours when I was too tired to read and had to just lay there. When I wasn't listening to my soft music, most of those afternoons were spent in silence as I stared at the ceiling, often looking out the window at the tree top near the house (and a bit of sky) or savouring the spiritual images at the foot of my bed. I was painfully aware that I was stuck alone in a basement while the world went on without me. Over time, I began feeling the sweetness of the calm and quiet solitude I was afforded through my condition. Again, my perspective shifted and I could see that I was accountable to no one. I was free to be who I am. This realisation would naturally bring me to a new challenge: Finding out who I am...

I listened to the silence and began to dig deeper, to let it speak to a place inside of me that had remained mostly hidden to me in spite of all my years of therapy and in spite of my extensive spiritual journey. I entered a new space that only silence can reveal. In this space, there is beauty, serenity, healing energy, love and yes, even happiness! This is who I am. I can chose to go to this very unique and private space at anytime and there, I find that pure living spark – my true self - that connects me to God. I carry the images that make up my secret garden and in the most difficult times – when and *if* I can remember to control my ego – I simply, by taking a few deep breaths, enter my inner sanctuary and almost instantly chase away all sorts of torment. But I must tell you that it does take a lot of practice.

The voice of aloneness cannot come from your head or ego, as I like to call my intellectual thought process. Ego is the voice of *loneliness*. It is a voice of sorrow, regret and anger that can send you in a state of deep despair. It takes you away to any place but where you are now, to another time, a happier time when you were healthy. Was there such a time?

As I searched over the events of my life, I was not surprised to see that I was never very happy. Sure, there were happy times, like when I studied theatre and was shining on stage, when my children were born or when I got my first horse.

Looking back today, one could say that I was living with undiagnosed and consequently untreated post-traumatic stress from early childhood experiences. Was it silently eating away at my body?

I spent time agonizing over the life I had lost, the life that could have been. I grieved for the woman I could have been in the world, and most painful of all, I grieved for the loss of my friends or those I thought of as friends. I felt sad that even those few friends I managed to keep were unavailable to me; they had their own issues, their own life and besides, most of them were now far away and didn't know about my situation. Yes, I could have made a phone call but

I figured they could have inquired about me if they wanted to know what had happened to me and why I had disappeared from their radar.

Listening to the loud voice of loneliness – when you believe every thought that crosses your mind - can sometimes weigh heavily on the heart. I learned to just let it be until it went away. Till the next pity party...

I worked hard to silence my ego so that I could just *be.* Only in the stillness of my mind, in peaceful solitude, could I sometimes hear the voice of my heart that was telling me that I was "enough", worthy and in the process of healing my life.

Humility and humour

I was on welfare for some months when I received a letter stating that the time had come for me to apply for a government disability pension. Much evaluation and paper work were involved in this most unpleasant process. Just for the record: First applications for disability income are generally always refused, no matter where you live. Then, you will contest their decision and will be sent forms to be completed by their experts, usually a psychiatrist and a rheumatologist, depending on the disability involved. That is what happened to me.

My first evaluation was with a psychiatrist. It was short and to the point. His job was to estimate if there was any reason – mental health wise - why I should not be able to work. Of course there wasn't. Then there was the visit to the rheumatologist.

It was hell. Not only was his office far from home, but Sarah (Who was feeling much better, driving me to most appointments but keeping an emotional distance.) and I waited for an hour before I was allowed into his office where I spent close to two hours. I answered the most intimate questions about how I spent my days, how I washed, dressed, ate, got groceries; he covered every detail of my existence until I got so weak that I told him I couldn't go on anymore and had to lie down *now*. The doctor had me lie down on his tiny examination table while he poked at me to see where my tender spots were; yep, fibromyalgia.

Back in his office, the stone-faced rheumatologist informed me that he only had a few more questions, only another 20 minutes. I wanted to die. I simply could not sit up anymore and told him to not mind me but that I was going to lie on the floor for the remainder of the interview. He sat up and leaned over to the other side of his desk to see me lying there with my legs on the chair at a 90-degree angle. He looked at me with a very slight expression of surprise and indifference. Then he continued with his questions. I was miserable and humiliated. The interview did finish on a positive note however. His final question was this: Is there any reason why you cannot go to work tomorrow?

Umm, really? The woman is on the floor for heaven's sake! The question seemed so ridiculous to me that I broke out in a roaring belly laugh. I laughed so hard it hurt. I was dizzy, flushed and hiccupped several times before regaining my composure. He just sat there and waited. I managed to get on my knees and lean on the edge of the desk facing him and said: 'I tell you what; I'll come and work for you tomorrow. Will you hire me?'

I did not get an answer. I did not get a thank you. Nada. Zip.

Four weeks later, I received a letter from the disability pensions' office stating that I was deemed well enough for a sedentary desk job (Which would have been OK I suppose, if I were allowed to bring a pillow and comforter and lie ON said desk all day...) and was not eligible for a disability pension. I was devastated. I was furious at the rheumatologist. After a few days of crying and feeling defeated, I picked up the phone and applied for legal aid; another long and gruelling process involving several trips for interviews.

I found the number of that lawyer who I had been referred to by my old fibromyalgia support group and who was known for winning disability cases like mine. I met with him a few times to go over my files and he responded to the disability pension agency thus: A CFS specialist has not yet evaluated my client for the purposes of her request for a disability pension. The two doctors who made their recommendations are not experts in this field and therefore are not apt to make any recommendation whatsoever as to my client's capacity to work. We ask that a CFS specialist whose name is included here, evaluate my client, and that you cover all costs related to this evaluation.

Legally, there was no other option, so they agreed. It was easy enough to get my specialist to fill out the evaluation form; she already knew about ME/CFS and about my particular level of disability. In a mere two weeks after her report was sent, I got a letter confirming that I was on disability, retroactive to 2004! Of course, I had to give most of the money back to welfare, but it felt good to be vindicated, to be believed.

From welfare to disability is not exactly a glamorous step up in the world. I had to put aside my pride more times in just a few years than ever before in my life and as the pride eroded, I discovered genuine humility.

I was at a point where I now knew that poverty has more to do with what you have in your heart than in your bank account. I have never felt poor since.

And as I was faced with the fact that my body was disabled, I began to re-evaluate my notions on that too. This sort of disability is mostly a physical limitation and I began to see that although my life had drastically changed because of it, I was still the same person, only wiser and less willing to pass

79

judgement on people who do not appear to contribute anything to the world.

As my heart started to open up, I began to feel better. I gave myself permission to take the needed time to get over the stress of the past few months and found *my* normal level of energy again. I felt optimistic about the future but did not look too far ahead. I focussed on each day and what I was able to do.

Then, two wonderful things happened almost simultaneously. My friend Sandra called and we got together for lunch. She was better and could talk about what had happened to her and where she was now. It felt so good to reconnect, to feel her friendship again, and to know that she was healing.

Just a few days later, I got a call from my daughter Sarah, who wanted to take me out for Sushi. She too was feeling better every day and was now going on interviews for work. I listened, as she was able to speak of the journey that had deeply changed her; I wanted to hold her in my arms. I ached for her. You never want to see your children go through painful times. But there was a distance between us that had not been there before and I respected that she needed time to fully mend. My own pain was something she was unable to hear about. She had put solid boundaries between herself and the parents who had betrayed her, at least in her view of the events that had occurred during her breakdown, i.e. spiritual awakening. As difficult as it was for me to accept this new distance between us, I rejoiced in the fact that Sarah was whole again and did want a relationship with me.

My role as mother had undergone major transformations in the last few years and I had to face the fact that although my children loved their mom, they had moved on and no longer needed me in a way that made me happy. I had to mourn the loss of the mother I could have been had I not had to deal with this illness.

We are all vulnerable creatures. We fall. We get up. We go on. I rejoice for those of us who repeat the process over and over with childlike trust in Life. I admire Sandra and Sarah: It is powerful and inspiring to witness silent, invisible heroic strength in a world that equates success with money and power.

It is a deeply humbling experience to search for your own worth when your life is lived in a tiny little corner of that big world in which you no longer feel you belong. And so I allow myself to also admire my own might. As I learned to manage the dragon while collecting precious insight, gratitude began to well up in my heart.

Chapter 6

Abundance and boundaries

It was now 2008. I'd been living with the dragon for 7 years. Deep in the heart of me, I have never doubted that I would someday heal and send him on his way.

In the meantime, I had learned to stop feeling sorry for myself, for the most part. Flare-ups no longer sent me in the depths of despair; I knew they would pass. I had translated a book, which made me feel useful. With careful planning, I could afford to purchase the supplements I needed and although I lived a frugal lifestyle, I lacked for nothing. I enjoyed Harry Potter and had experienced the publishing of the last two books; so much fun and excitement, which I shared with my online community. My daughters took me to see the movies when they came out and I would go see them again with Julie. I have since, read the series of books at least six times and seen the movies enough times to qualify as a Harry Potter nerd. To this day, when I feel upset or tense, I watch one of the DVDs. Needless to say I'm somewhat of an expert on the subject and I would go so far as saying that the boy wizard saved my life.

You have my gratitude Madame Rowling. The world that you put on paper with so much artistry, so much knowledge of human nature and with such a tremendous amount of love, opened my heart to a magic I had left behind as I grew up. In my darkest hour, I found the hero in me. I reconnected with magic once more and experienced a joy that lifted me up and allowed me to soar again! "I love magic." is my favourite quote from the Harry Potter films because it says it all. Try saying it and you will feel a little something stir inside your heart. That's where the magic lives.

Now sharing an apartment in the city, my daughters wanted me to move closer to them. Things were set in motion although the prospect of moving again was scary. Jessie and I began to increase our walking time and I felt better than I had in years although I was far from cured. I had found a new normal that I could be comfortable with. By keeping a daily log of my pain and energy levels, I could now see patterns which allowed me a sense of empowerment in the knowledge that there were aspects of this illness that I could somewhat control and manage. For example, I knew that going out for errands caused me a lot of pain afterwards, so I took pain medication before going out. I also made sure that I did not stand in line too long anywhere because I knew that I would feel very weak if I did.

Since that visit to the rheumatologist, I have been known to lie on the floors of a few clinics and even a hospital waiting room. I cannot sit up for very long either – it is called orthostatic intolerance. It likely has to do with the fact that ME patients have difficulty metabolising oxygen and the brain can easily get starved if one is in a vertical position for too long. No one knows for sure. This is just one of the nearly sixty symptoms of ME, of which I have about half in varying degrees of severity. In my earlier ME/CFS evaluations, the degree of my illness was classified as severe. By 2008 (and to this day), based on my levels of incapacity, pain and energy, I was somewhere between moderate and severe.

I began sorting things out in my tiny apartment and managed to purge some stuff I really didn't need after all. I gave away more clothing and small kitchen appliances along with various knick-knacks. It is amazing how one can simplify their life by having fewer things to carry around and to dust. I became more and more aware of what really mattered to me.

One day, Amy and I found the perfect little 2½-basement apartment only two blocks from where my girls lived. Well, perfect is a bit of an exaggeration. The place had potential but the owner of the triplex in which it was located had neglected it. OK, it was far from perfect, and when Sandra drove me there on the day I was to sign the lease, she took one look and said: 'No way my friend is living here!' The owner was startled as was I, by the boldness of her comment. So she took us on a, well, very short tour. The kitchen cabinets were in a bad state on the inside, and there were visible signs of water damage under the sink. Mould is risky for anyone's health and tenfold for those of us with immune issues.

Except for the kitchen, there was nothing that couldn't be fixed and because Sandra knew how much the location, price and overall advantages of the place meant to me, she made the owner a deal he couldn't refuse. She would tear down the kitchenette, clean up the mould and rebuild a brand new one. This, along with a few other modifications to the place, she would do for literally half of what it would have cost in materials alone! Both the owner and I were thrilled. And as I signed the lease, she told him that he better take good care of his new tenant because he was getting a great one on top of the improvements to his apartment which he could eventually rent for a higher price when I would move out.

And so began two months of packing and sorting. One or two boxes a day was all I could manage. My girls came over one day and helped pack up the kitchen. Meanwhile Sandra and her carpenter boyfriend renovated my new place. How great is that? What wonderful generosity! When the time came, Sarah and Amy went over to clean and scrub the bathroom, wash windows and began to paint. Sandra, knowing my preferred colors, created a

85

beautiful and peaceful environment for me. By the time March 1ˢᵗ came around, I had moved-in with the help of my daughters and their friends. I felt at home right away. Jessie could be let out through my bedroom window and access a patch of grass on the side of the building, near the quiet street (by city standards of course).

All was well. I was thoroughly exhausted and extremely grateful for all the help and the gifts I had been given. The day after I moved, we were hit with a huge snowstorm. Although my landlord was responsible for snow removal, by the time his worker had gotten around to my entrance, three days had gone by. My girls had to come and clear the window I needed to let Jessie out and they shovelled like mad to make sure we could get my car moved to the other side of the street as per city regulations. They were actually happy about the situation, knowing that they didn't have to drive long distances when I needed their help.

Another two months later, I finally unpacked the last of the boxes from the move. I got to enjoy the summer by sitting in the sun a bit and by discovering my new neighbourhood with Jessie. Every week or so, I walked over to the girls' apartment to do my laundry; I no longer had access to a washer/dryer. I would spend most of the day there watching TV while they were at work, and doing a couple of loads of laundry for them too. I cleaned up their kitchen a bit and washed the stack of dishes in the sink of these busy working ladies. When they didn't get home in time to drive me back to my place, I would walk back with Jessie and one of them would drop by the next day with my clean laundry. We had a great arrangement and I was so happy to get to see them more often, sometimes for a bite of lunch or a short outing.

I walked a new walk and felt more secure. I decided to apply for a handicapped-parking vignette after going to the nearby mall one day, and seeing two young women cut me off to take my parking space before walking away laughing. Going to the mall is gruelling enough without having to walk a long distance to and from the car. I still use my vignette today and it is a great help to me. I deserve it. Anyone living with a dragon does.

Although I had sworn decades ago that I would never live in the city again, I found a way to make it work. After all, except for my walks with Jessie, I didn't go out that often. I was happy to discover a park just a street away, where I could sit while Jessie sniffed around or lay in the sun. I found trees there and they made me happy although this setting being less private, I did not hug them!

I resumed my daily routine and life went on. I couldn't go to the food bank in the city; it was too far and just too big for me, and it was regulated and organised for the healthy. One of my daughters began making a monthly deposit on my credit card and it was a lifesaver. Both my daughters have helped me several times over the years, either by bringing me homemade food, treating me to a movie, a restaurant or buying me clothes. It's crazy when you think about it. They were in their twenties; it really should have been me helping my children. I couldn't get that thought out of my mind... I did the best I could to repay them by listening and sharing a laugh when they occasionally wanted me to be there for them.

Such as it was, I could see that my life was blessed with abundance at every turn. The universe practically met all of my needs.

This was never so clear as in January of 2009. One morning, Jessie woke up listless and refused food. I waited, figuring that now 10 years old, she could just be having an off day. I let her out the next morning after she ate a bit. She saw the kids next door and she got all excited and ran toward them to play. Then it happened. She keeled over. She was out a few seconds then got up as I shouted her name and tugged at the rope to which she was tied. Amy drove me to the vet within 30 minutes and an hour later, we learned that Jessie had a severe case of Auto-Immune Hemolytic Anemia. And an x-ray showed that she had a small bullet lodged in her chest, near her shoulder; it broke our hearts to know just how much that little dog must have suffered before I adopted her from a shelter when she was 2 years old.

Prednisone was prescribed to stop her immune system from destroying her few remaining red blood cells. It would be a long journey to recovery *if* she recovered. We were told chances were slim considering her age. That morning's event had been a heart attack, and another one would likely be fatal. To avoid that probability, I would have to carry her outside to do her business and make sure nothing would disturb her. No doorbell ringing, no visitors.

Back home that night, as she lay on her side in her bed, barely conscious, I whispered to her that it was OK to go if she was too tired; I thanked her for the joy she had given me at a time when I badly needed reasons to smile. Then later, before going to sleep, I prayed that she would get better, asking God to leave her with me a while longer. I felt so alone and had let go of so much already; I wasn't ready to say goodbye now.

As I fussed over a very sick Jessie for several months, I realized why we had chosen each other. We are two of a kind. We have both endured prolonged stress early in life; we had suffered from the effects of post-traumatic stress (In my case, before the term existed). When the immune system fails to do its job, it is often the result of years of adrenaline-producing fear and anguish. I thought about that day when we met and marvelled at how she had somehow sensed that we were destined to help each other heal. She had chosen me.

By summer, thanks to the generosity of my children (Without whom I would have had to put Jessie down.) and the wholehearted dedication of the veterinary staff, against all odds, Jessie made a full recovery. She still had so much life in her!

She was once again my personal trainer and a joyful inspiration on my own path to wellness.

How my life was filled with abundance! I now knew deep down, how it felt for the first time ever.

With all the information I've read on the Internet over the years, after talking to other ME patients, reading a fair number of scientific papers written by the foremost experts on the subject and attending lectures through support organisations, I learned that many people with this illness have suffered some kind of trauma during childhood. Whether sexual, physical or verbal in nature, or all of the above, a prolonged stressor such as abuse and/or neglect is likely to diminish immune response in a child. It is often a life sentence.

This common denominator leads me to believe that one of the ways to repair the damage that was done not only to the body, but also to the heart or the soul if you will, is to become aware of the concept of boundaries. As I know from personal experience, children of abuse have been taught that they have no line of defence or limits as far as their person is concerned. They are subject to the abuser's whims and there is nothing they can do about it. They live, often year after year, in a state of fight or flight even if the abuse occurred on one single occasion. They grow up not as individuals that are part of a community where they can feel safe, but as lonely prey forever on the alert, never quite fitting in wherever they go.

It can take many years of therapy or counselling of some sort to alter the perception that one is a prey, a victim, a being unworthy of love, unable to trust anyone, including himself or herself. It is impossible to trust our own self when we have not acquired a sense of boundary, when we cannot say 'enough' or 'no'. We often grow up as people pleasers, over achievers, charmers and very, very, needy.

Living with a dragon has taught me to set my boundaries.

After all, whether I want to or not, I frequently have to say 'No, I can't do this'. One of the most effective steps on the path of healing is to explore a place *within* where you begin to allow yourself the right to just *be*. This, I believe, is a very difficult thing to do. It involves letting go of judgement, including self-criticism; two behaviours at which we are very adept.

In the many lonely hours I've spent in bed, I heard the thoughts of my ego in my mind. It has told me a million times that I am worthless and useless, just lying there. It really is this voice that keeps us down in the dumps, as if we didn't have enough to deal with, having an incurable illness. I read somewhere that incurable really means curable from the _in_side. Fascinating isn't it? What if this is true? Forget about the "it's all in your head" nonsense and let's dig deeper. Yes, the voice of the ego is in our head but it only has the amount of power we are willing to hand over. All those thoughts going through our mind need to be questioned! Are they *really* true?

From what I understand, the ego is the voice that relives the past and projects into the future. It is the voice of all the pain we carry in our subconscious and that has taken up residence in every cell of our body. It is the voice of all the dreams we will never see come true. It is a composite of all the voices from our childhood. While we unconsciously pursue happiness, our ego gets a more powerful grip on our life and things get out of control. This is true for the sick, the healthy, the young and the old. If you're human, you have an ego that has formed your personality and self-image. It has given you a vision of the world that makes sense to you until, when you change your state of consciousness, it doesn't anymore.

The ego is not the enemy; it only needs to be under our control and not the other way around.

How to get back control over our life, our health and happiness? We could start with a couple of strategies. First, not believing everything we think. Second, awakening our consciousness and listening to the voice of our true *self*, our authentic self which lives in only one place: Here and now.

So, for me, the ideal way of learning to set boundaries was to begin to tell my ego to be quiet. Yes, we have to work at quieting the mind. Whatever means you prefer is fine. I like to listen to guided meditation. It certainly beats just lying there feeling sorry for myself...

When the mind becomes quiet, the ego's voice cannot be heard. As mind and body relax, we begin to release the accumulated stress that has prevented healing from happening. Over time, I have learned to *catch* my ego and I quickly tell it to be quiet. When I start thinking unhappy thoughts or when fearful images come up, I remind myself that this is not how I choose to spend my precious energy, that this is not true and not what I want to be thinking about.

Setting boundaries for my ego is an ongoing work and as I get better at it, I can set boundaries in my relationships with others.

It is still difficult to say 'no' because I'm feeling unwell physically, when emotionally, I would love to say 'yes'. I would love to go to a girl's night out in town. I simply can't manage to sit for two hours on a cute bistro chair in a noisy restaurant, near an air vent... Never mind the drive! 'Oh you don't have to drive, I'll come pick you up'. What a nice offer, but *normals* just don't understand that by the time I've showered, dressed, put on some make-up and combed my hair, I am already exhausted even if these actions have been spread out over the entire day with rest periods in between.

Another factor to consider is the actual drive, even as a passenger. The movement of the car puts additional stress on my system, which has to deal with visual distortions and vertigo issues. Sometimes, I do participate in a gathering that I can handle but there is always, always, a price to pay! Remember PEM for post exertion malaise (There are other terms for this.)? When friends or family go back to their usual activities, we get to lie down for days just to get back *our* normal level of energy.

Setting boundaries is of utmost importance for those on the path to wellness. It is an essential part of managing, not just illness, but life in general.

Those who care about us also have limits.

As I learned to ask for help, I became aware of people's reactions. At first, when I was so desperately ill, it was difficult for me to notice anything outside of my own experience, my own body. But I eventually started sensing that my now ex-husband began to withdraw emotionally. I felt no resentment from him, just cold, calm, unemotional responses and behaviour. This made me realise that he was unable to deal with the situation and didn't know what to do except act out of self-preservation. To be honest, I didn't come to that realisation before going through feelings of hurt, desolation, abandonment and anger. We had taken vows just a few short years ago and were getting along fairly well before the illness. How could he do this to me? The answer lay in his own boundaries, which he was painfully becoming to terms with.

When my friend Sandra moved me to an environment conductive to healing, she gave me all she could until she could no longer be there for me, for a long period of time. It was extremely difficult for me to accept that she had reached her limit so soon.

As for my daughters, to this day, they both do their best to be supportive and understanding. For almost a decade, on several occasions, they drove me to doctors' appointments and tended to many of my countless calls for help. But there came a point when they began to express their frustrations. They felt that I didn't care about their life, their time, their limits. They had ignored their boundaries in a genuine effort to help their mother, but it created resentment that seeped into our relationship and created tensions.

We have so few close relationships when struggling with chronic illness, that it is imperative that we make every effort to become supportive and understanding toward others as well. I was forced to open my eyes to the fact that my daughters and my friends cared for me very much, but they also had to set their boundaries if we were to have a relationship of equal value for all involved. I had to learn to accept a 'no' to some requests without feeling rejected or hurt. I had to acknowledge the limits of the people I love because although mine are many, theirs are just as real and just as important to them as mine are to me.

An invisible illness often solicits little support or sympathy from people we encounter occasionally. Neighbours for instance, will listen to your story and "understand" your situation but will think nothing of having a New Year's Eve party 'till 4am without so much as a word to inform you in advance, so that you can arrange to sleep elsewhere on that night instead of suffering through hours of loud music and partying. They don't care? Maybe. But it is more likely that they are nice folks who just don't get it or they simply forgot, or they didn't think their music was that loud. Whatever the reason, it is kinder to our self and to others, not to assume anything. The fact is simply that every one has limits, limitations or healthy boundaries!

PART TWO

Chapter 7

Embracing the illness

It was Mother Teresa who said something to the effect
that she would not get involved *against* anything,
but if she were asked to manifest or speak up *for* a
cause, then she would be happy to consider it. I have
always felt that way too.

In this frame of mind, I find it difficult to join in
the *fight* against cancer or any number of illnesses,
including ME. I never really had a desire to fight
against a *dis*-ease I've been living with since 2001.
There is a part of my body that is telling me that I
must awaken to something that still eludes me and
I strive to open-up my state of consciousness every
single day. I'd say 'every single moment', but I'm not
quite there yet. Far from it.

I trust my body today and I listen. I have learned
that our body already possesses the ability to heal

all illnesses, so I have no reason to fight anything inside of me. On the contrary, I believe the last thing an immune system that has been on high alert for decades needs, is another fight.

Not to offend anyone, but I don't want to be a warrior. That, however, does not mean that won't stand up for myself, for other patients and for our cause!

As much as I struggled to get well in the beginning, as much as I rebelled against my situation and cried over it, I just felt worse, not better. After a couple of years, it occurred to me that perhaps, the best strategy was to again, let go. A chronic illness, above all, teaches us to let go. We are subjected to loss of such huge proportions that there comes a time where we either give up or give in.

If, like me, you are not one to give up, then we could ask our self: what is the meaning of giving in? For me, it has been a process through which I have learned *acceptance*. Accepting my condition brought me a sense of peace: OK, there's a dragon by my side 24/7. Now what? I chose to stop thinking and saying that this is wrong, not normal, certainly not fair, and 'why me?' I began by taking a step back and looking at my situation from a different perspective. If, for some reason, I was going to live this way for who knows how long, I had to make some sense of it. I had to give my life a new meaning that I had not planned on exploring.

I decided to use the life-coaching and management skills I knew so well, having used them to help others in my past professional life. I took out a notebook and began writing answers to such questions as:

- What defines me? (Hint: Make a list of your values. For example: Integrity, peace, health, joy, etc.)
- What is my most important value?
- By what concrete actions can I *be/embody* that value in my everyday life?

This may not seem like much; however, it is the beginning of getting to know who we really are. Try it! Here is an example of a value that is translated into concrete actions:

Value: Respect

Statement for daily actions:

1. <u>I *am* Respect when</u> I stop doing whatever I'm doing when I feel the need to rest.
2. <u>I *am* Respect when</u> I give my family time to adjust and I accept that they do not entirely get it.
3. <u>I *am* respect when</u> I take time to tell myself that I appreciate my resilience and courage.

As you become more adept at actualizing your value, you can add others and continue the process. You will eventually discover that all values point to Love.

Love is who you really are! This is the *you* that you can embrace and truly cherish.

You will find that on some days, you are not doing so well at incarnating your values. In this process of self-discovery, there are three other components that will help you move forward on your journey:

1. Taking risks. Allow yourself to move out of your comfort zone by ignoring fears and feelings of guilt. Do what you set out to do, even if it's just a little step toward your goal.
2. Appreciation. At the end of the day, write in your notebook at least three things you appreciate in you. (Ex: I am so proud that I folded the laundry today!) Celebrate; treat yourself to something that makes you smile, like calling a friend, hugging your pet, or watching your favourite program and yes you can invite Ben&Jerry to join the celebration!
3. Learning something. We may not stop and take notice but we can learn something valuable from every single experience. As you try out this little process, see if you can write down something that you have become aware of and that raises your spirits. For example, if you would normally feel in the dumps because you were unable to do what you set out to accomplish, you can look for a positive lesson, like: Today, I learned that I want to set more attainable goals.

You will notice that the positive things you learn bring you back to your values. You can continue this process – it is a fun way to keep a diary - over and over. You will notice that it will bring you full circle to the real you; the you that you want to know.

In a surprisingly short time, you will begin to feel the emergence of authentic self-acceptance. You've read it before: You are not your illness. Now, you can really begin to feel that you are not your illness. Look back at your notes, your values and accomplishments, the courage and resilience that you can be proud of every single day, and you will see the evidence that you are much more than your physical limitations!

For me, there came a time when I would allow myself a pity party without feeling worthless. I have the right to get sick and tired of feeling sick and tired. We all do. That being said and accepted, we can perhaps take it a step further and look in the mirror and say: 'You know what? I think you're wonderful!' This is the beginning of *embracing* yourself as you are. Embracing the illness is simply embracing yourself as a worthy person who happens to have to manage an illness. All humans have issues. This dragon can certainly be the biggest one for us.

I began to reach deeper inside myself, observing my thoughts and the sensations in my body, as well as my feelings. As I slowly allowed myself to embrace all of me without judgement, I noticed that feelings of guilt and worthlessness gradually faded. I went from 'this is my fault' to: 'I take full responsibility for all that I am.'

I want to clarify a very important notion: responsibility.

All of us are responsible for our own life and everything in it. This statement can be very empowering if you understand that there is no connotation of guilt involved here. I am responsible for my illness. All of the choices I have made in my human experience have led me to where I am. I believe there is no such thing as coincidence. I believe that the universe works in perfect order in spite of our best efforts to override its magnificence.

This being said, if I am responsible for my illness, I am also responsible for my healing. Nothing stays the same. The universe is constantly changing, moving, growing and evolving. We are part of this universe. In fact, wiser and more enlightened people than me would say that we ARE the universe: it flows through us and we are but one drop in the cosmic ocean of infinite possibilities! Remember?

You may be tempted to push this aside as 'New Age' stuff, but please take a moment to let it sink in: At every moment, we have at hand the power of a universe in which our bodies are programmed to be healthy. We all have the same potential for health. It is up to us to *allow* the healing to flow through us.

Embracing the illness and the whole of our being is a wonderful way of releasing the heavy baggage – resentments, old grudges, guilt... mostly limiting, useless thoughts and beliefs - that stands in the way of radiant health and happiness.

Out there

I had been living on my own for four years when it became clear to me that I wanted someone to share my life with, someone to love, to be intimate with. I didn't know how to go about it or if there even existed a man who would actually want to live with a woman dealing with ME.

There are different takes on chronic illness. Many people make light of invisible illnesses; sadly many of them are doctors. A few years ago, in an attempt to create some awareness, best selling author Laura Hillenbrand (Seabiscuit, Unbroken) wrote something to the effect that *being tired is to ME what a match is to a nuclear bomb.* She has had ME all of her adult life, so I consider her an expert on the subject, as are all of us managing a dragon. She also has to deal with the painful fact that we do not *look* sick but are nevertheless, often seriously disabled.

With that in mind, I wondered if I had the energy and the courage to put myself out there... I eventually did start dating after finally deciding to join an Internet dating site for people over 50. I met a man who also had ME. It was a wonderful experience to spend time with another person who had a front row seat into the life we are confined to lead. Interestingly, this man who was a couple years younger than I was, had a completely different attitude towards his illness. It was interesting but it was a chore for me. This person took absolutely no responsibility for his life and was a victim of circumstances over which he had no control. We did have empathy and understanding for each other's pains and limitations but our compatibility ended there so after a few months, I put an end to the relationship. I learned that having the same illness is no guaranty that we see it the same way.

So, I continued perusing my chosen Internet dating site and began to have email exchanges with a few men who found me interesting enough in spite of my health issue. Eventually, some of those graduated to phone calls and some to actual coffee dates. Dating was exhilarating and scary and fun. Feeling attractive, interesting and wanted is very good for morale and I highly recommend putting yourself out there if you can, even if it does take a lot of energy. I never lied about my illness but I also did not over dramatize it. Many men were put off by it and I expected that, so I didn't take it personally. Others felt protective and were very attentive towards me.

I met a very handsome man with whom I had carried-on a telephone relationship due to the fact that he was vacationing abroad at the time. Throughout that summer, he called me almost every day and we had a chance to talk about a multitude of subjects during our long conversations. We were very eager to meet, seeing that we had so many ideologies, tastes and other things in common. I remember the first time we met in a fancy restaurant near my home. I was smitten. He had beautiful blue eyes and a lovely mane of silvery hair that made me want to swoon. He seemed equally taken by me. In no time at all, we were seeing each other on a regular basis. And, yes, it was too good to be true... The man was everything I wanted except for the fact that he was very controlling and my level of stress kept increasing with every encounter. Definitely no good for my health. I ended it. Felt bad about it. Got over it.

I kept going out on occasional coffee dates, most of which didn't pan out for a variety of reasons. But the experience was beneficial for me, so I kept at it.

Finally it paid off. I met a lovely man, a real gentleman who would become my life partner. JR was a full-time music teacher. He had been a professional musician since his teens, had toured all over the US and later became a songwriter and music producer. Besides teaching, he was leading a jazz band that played in small venues, had recorded his own CD and had begun writing a book.

JR is ten years older than me. Perhaps the age difference was a factor in his acceptance of my limitations. He, himself, was dealing with pain issues so he understood the chronic aspects of an illness that keeps on going for who knows how long. Our relationship evolved naturally, without the 'falling in love' bolt of lightning phenomenon.

We just immediately felt comfortable in each other's company. There were adjustments of course, but we both had needs that seemed to be filled by being in each other's presence.

We became very close and a year and a half later, we decided to move in together. Since he was cutting down his workweek by one day each year heading for retirement, we had a pretty tight budget with only old age pensions ahead of us. So, I began to look at subsidised housing for 55 year-olds and over. My dream was to move back to the mountains that I so loved and we made a plan that would get us there in four years. Until then, JR had to live in the city, fairly close to his workplace. We found a housing co-op that offered us the opportunity to put aside enough money each year so that we could eventually rent north of the city with the basic comforts and a modest nest egg.

JR went to visit the housing project and met with the coordinator who showed him a fairly nice apartment that was clean and surrounded by trees and a park. Jessie was welcome too. It sounded too good to be true. Right. JR was very enthusiastic about the place and the price, although he had reservations about the neighbourhood and the neighbours. The project had buildings for seniors, but no apartments were available there at the time, so we were offered a unit in a six-apartment block occupied by families. On the day I went to visit, everything was quiet and we were assured that nice, quiet people occupied this building. We made my health issues very clear and emphasised that our priority was to live in as little stress as possible. No problem, they assured us.

I had noticed that JR, like many artists, is unusually intuitive and very sensitive. On the day that we went to sign the lease for the apartment, we had a bit of an argument. He wanted to back out because he had a bad feeling about the place. I got annoyed and frustrated and a fair bit angry as we sat in the car in front of the offices at the low cost housing co-op and he changed his mind! He now wanted to rent a much more expensive apartment we had previously visited and that would use up all our resources.

After all was said and done, he got out of the car and said 'OK, let's go in and sign the lease'. My heart was beating in my throat and I felt faint so I told him the energy was all wrong and that it would not be a good idea to sign now. He insisted, apologised and soft-talked me into getting out of the car. We signed the papers on that day that would catapult us into a valuable learning experience.

So, again, I began sorting and packing. I sold some of my furniture to the next tenant who was renting my small bachelor pad. I paced myself but still got terrible flare-ups that put be in bed, scared and helpless. I got a bit of help from my daughters, but I must say that by that time (This was my third move in five years.), I was beginning to wear out their generosity. They were happy that I had found someone to share my life with and I knew they were glad that it would take some of the load off their shoulders. It did, but they still were asked again to help with painting and moving. I took no part in that phase and thankfully, I was pleased to learn that the girls liked JR and that it was mutual.

Shortly after we moved in, our hell began. A 350-pound man lived in the apartment above and rose at 4am to go to work. The floors creaked so badly that we were awakened every day and could rarely go back to sleep due to the fact that at 6:30am, the kids in the block started running around, getting ready for school or daycare. I was shocked to find out that there were a total of ten kids ranging from 1½ to 13 years old in our unit. It was bedlam. Our days were disturbed by shouting and door slamming, running in the echoing hallways, playing in said hallways without adult supervision. Hell!

I tried to modify the situation by opening my door and telling the kids to play in their home or outside, to stop yelling in the hall, to shut their door gently, but to no avail. We talked to the man living above us. He told us to get earplugs, which we did, to no avail. He did not care. To make matters worse, his very pregnant girlfriend moved in with him along with his morbidly obese, disabled sister. One day, the father of one of the kids I had spoken to, came to me in a rage, forbidding me to EVER speak to his children again and to move out if I wasn't happy. Another man literally threatened me and assaulted me verbally without even looking at me; addressing his aggression to JR who remained calm and did not throw oil on the fire.

My level of stress was way over what I could stand, so I was often knocked out with flare-ups, crying. JR was as stressed out as I was and he tried his best to keep my spirits up. But it was clear that our intuitions and disagreement on the day of the signing of the lease had been signs to which we would have been better off paying attention. Choosing to listen to intellect instead of intuition is not a good idea.

After fourteen months of misery, we were allowed to break our lease and move out. This time, we did everything together, took our time and I managed to flare-up only once for a few days during the whole moving period. We finally moved into a freshly painted apartment – in the colors of our choosing - in a suburb north of the city; it was a step in the right direction as far as our plans to eventually move to the mountains.

By the time we had completely settled in our new place, not only had we depleted our savings, but also we were now paying a lot more for rent. We had been living together for a year and a half under extreme stress. Our relationship was still harmonious for the most part, but our life together had been difficult to say the least. The housing project had been our school of hard knocks. Having worked on the unpacking for most of the summer, we were looking forward to enjoying the badly needed peace we so deserved.

We lived above the owners of a duplex. They had two teenage children and a big, gorgeous dog named

Molly. Imagine our disheartening shock when September came and the dog, now left alone all day, began to howl and bark for hours each day! When we brought up the problem, we were told that they never had a complaint about this before (Naturally, if their previous tenants were at work...) and that there was nothing they could do now that the kids were back in school.

The problem somewhat decreased in intensity as the dog adapted, as *we* adapted. We went back to living with earplugs for naptime or when we wanted a break from the noise. The upside was that the neighbourhood was quiet and we had peaceful evenings.

We also could sleep past 4am.

Chapter 8

About forgiveness

When I look at my life, it is easy to find a common denominator in almost all of the pain and hardships I have known: Judgment, fear and resentment; in other words, *my own ego.* I had resented my mother for decades. As a child, I loved and hated her with equal passion. I later allowed myself to pass judgement on her out of a sense of entitlement. I was the injured party and felt that the heavy wounds I carried grew out of her failure to be the mother I had needed and still needed. This attitude of judgement, entitlement and righteousness was inevitably turned toward myself and all who were part of my world. Because I believed that I was my story, I saw the world from the perspective of a deeply wounded and frightened child that would not be ignored or silenced.

After all the therapy I had gone through by the age of fifty, I still could not stand to be in the same room with my mother without feeling mutinous, very judgemental, frustrated and resentful.

By now however, my desire and willingness to forgive became increasingly powerful and I read more books in order to better understand the process of forgiveness. When illness struck, my priority had become survival. It became clear to me that my life urgently needed to become free of stress if I had any chance of healing and that meant that because I was unable to forgive, I could not have contact with my mother. We were in a mutually toxic relationship which I had severed many times over the years, attempting again and again to include her in my life. Part of me wanted my mother to love me. To just love me unconditionally, the way I love my own children.

By the time I had to leave Luc, I told her that I was very ill and wanted no contact with her. I stood by that decision for six years in spite of her attempts at phone conversations. I refused to have anything to do with her and politely told her so before hanging up the phone.

I understood the ravages that resentment had done to me. If I was abused as a child, it was short-lived compared to the abuse I had inflicted on myself as an adult.

I began to understand states of awareness; my own and that of others. I define awareness as a deep knowing that is life-transforming. It is being present to life and self *in the moment*. (See Eckart Tolle's works in the Resources section.)

I became aware of the pain I was causing my mother by refusing to accept her as she was. Whatever she had done in the past was over and done with and my responsibility to change lay in the moment. I had had enough of pain and toxic resentment! I began to look for qualities in my mother so that I could refocus my thoughts on a more positive frequency, so to speak. Without her actual presence to distract me from my goal, I envisioned her as the intelligent and artistic person she actually was. She was a very good painter and her taste in fashion and décor was impeccable. She was extremely social and loved to entertain and shine. Beauty was obviously her most important value. Nothing wrong with that!

Through the many hours during which I contemplated my life, I meditated on my own awareness. I began to accept without judgement – OK, with *less* judgement – that people had different states of awareness and that their actions came from a perception that was unique.

I thought about my first husband, my mother and my best friend Denise who, I felt had also cruelly betrayed me years ago. I needed to forgive these people most of all. But the resentment was still firmly held by my ego, that part of me that makes up the stories to which I cling to in order to feel justified and righteous. As time went by, I did realise that in order to feel real one must listen to that other voice, that of the soul: the true self who knows only love and peace because that *is* the nature of self! The nature of ego is illusion and suffering.

I did practice mastering my ego at times, but my transition to awareness of the *self* was far from complete. Is it ever, for anyone? All spiritual teachings bring us back to the ultimate act of living: breathing. I remembered that becoming aware of breathing is the first step in silencing the ego because it does not live in the present. It only knows the past and the fears and imaginings of the future. So I began to focus on breathing but this time, I had no agenda; I asked nothing more of myself. I easily let go of my guilt and frustration at my inability to forgive, knowing full well that this was a significant part of healing. I accepted and embraced the idea that I was preparing to allow myself the freedom of forgiveness.

For some people the process takes quite a bit of time. I began by forgiving myself for taking so long to forgive others. I understood that this was not going to be a one-time thing; it had to come from thoroughly, deeply, completely *letting go*. It had to become an attitude, a natural way to approach life with an open heart, a forgiving heart.

I still had a long way to go but life always provides the needed experiences to help us on our chosen journey.

The most important person

People dealing with a mostly invisible chronic illness make an assumption that everyone with whom they have a relationship, whether personal or professional, will understand that they are sick.

This is a source of much pain and frustration because the reality is that it is highly likely that if you have a chronic illness and don't look sick, you will not be treated any differently than if you were in perfect health.

A man I used to be friends with even told me that he would not enable me in my belief that I was ill! He would not accept doing all the driving if we were to go out for a movie or take a walk by the river. Needless to say that we are no longer friends... That's the way it goes with most of the people in our life; either we accept that they don't get it and never will, or the relationship ends, as is often the case.

I had a lot of difficulty wrapping my head around the fact that my family and friends didn't seem to know just how difficult it is to live the way I do! Why on earth would anybody choose such a life? Yes, I know about supplements; in fact, I could give a course on them! No, exercise is not going to help me; in fact, it may just kill me! It used to feel good to hear someone say how nice I looked. Now, it's almost an insult because I sense that they are saying: "You must *feel* nice too! So glad to see that you are getting better. ☺" No, I am not anywhere near better! In fact, each day is a new experience in pain, isolation and endless work. Yes, I work and I work hard. I have a new mountain to climb every single day and while I do push to reach my – what to *normals* would be menial - goals, I work at keeping frustration at bay. I work at keeping my ego and my dragon... in check and embracing, embracing, embracing my life as I strive to see the blessings in being able to accomplish the simple task of folding laundry.

Breathe. Just breathe.

It is imperative for us to deeply understand that each individual is the center of his or her own universe. It is only then that we can begin to accept that we are not on other people's mind 24/7. We are briefly on their radar some of the time. I truly believe that my remaining friends and grown children do not think of me every single day. If I'm honest, I don't think of them every day and if they happen to call me at an inconvenient time, it bothers me sometimes, although not as much as not getting that call at all!

Embracing self-care is for everyone, not just those of us who have an illness. All humans need to be valued and understood.

I learned this lesson a few years ago at Christmas time. Not my favourite holiday by far as I'm sure you can relate to the overwhelming expenditure of our precious energy that is required for social gatherings. My daughter Amy had moved into a brownstone in the city with her boyfriend, JJ. The building had several tenants and was co-owned by the boyfriend and his father. His family was often there to help out with renovations and improvements to the building. JJ's parents had become quite at home in my daughter's new living space. Anyway, she decided to decorate their living room with Holiday cheer and to invite her sister and boyfriend, along with JR and me for Christmas dinner. She planned it so both families could get acquainted and for us to see her new home for the first time. Sarah had been there several times already.

It was clear to me when we entered that JJ's parents were on their turf and the only guests were JR and I. JJ's sibling was there too and his stuff was all set up in the guest room along with the parent's belongings. We were not invited to sleep over. There was no room. And that, in spite of the fact that it was my first visit and that the one-hour drive had been very taxing for me. Thoughts began running through my mind... I had previously asked Amy to explain my condition to everyone present at the festivities. How could no one think of having me stay the night? How could anyone not know that the long Christmas supper would be very uncomfortable for me and that sitting through – what would turn out to be a two hour marathon – the opening of gifts would be totally exhausting for someone in my condition?

I felt like a stranger in my daughter's home. She took JR and I on a tour and was proud to show us the work they'd done. I was genuinely happy for her and made sure she knew it. Back in the kitchen where it would have been fun to take part in some light preparation work, I was left sitting and watching as JJ's mother helped my daughter prepare the meal. The woman was orchestrating things and it was clear that I was not to be involved. It hurt. I was a guest. This did not bother JR; the men were in the living room having animated conversation.

I had a nice time at supper and enjoyed my daughters' and grandchild's company, ignoring the pain and the exhaustion as we all must do in such circumstances. Before the end of supper, I had to get up and go sit in the annexed living room. I found a slightly more comfortable place to catch my breath while the others finished their wine and cheese. I noticed a mountain of gifts around the small tree and hoped that they were going to keep some for Christmas morning.

It was not to be.

I had also brought gifts for my kids and a token for JJ's parents. It must have been around 9pm when the opening of the gifts began. I got up several times to change seat. I was extremely tired by that time and most uncomfortable. I watched for over an hour as JJ's parents showered their children with so many gifts that I couldn't believe my eyes. Why would I want to witness their darlings get a pair of socks, gloves, a hat, another pair of socks, thermal underwear and who remembers what else?! I signalled JR that it was time to go. He came over and said we hadn't given our gifts yet. I waited. Feeling my heart pounding frantically against my ribs.

I began sweating profusely and felt as if I would faint any second. These people had been informed that I was sick, however, they did not let that change their plans. I changed mine! I let the evening go on to the point of a major crash. I finally could take it no more and got up as if I were drunk and said: 'I'm going to lie down now before I die.'

I staggered to Amy and JJ's room and crashed on their bed, gasping for air. JR and Amy rushed in after me. Amy said I ruined everybody's goodtime with my drama. I was so full of resentment towards these people that I couldn't have cared less. *I* ruined *their* evening? I bet that if I had been in a wheelchair, or blind, they would have made adjustments to accommodate me!

I was in tears and wanted to go home. I felt bad for my family who wanted to give me their gifts, so I got up, put on a smile and walked back into the living room. 'Sorry', I said. JJ's mother said we'd get to our family's gifts so I could leave. We did and I did.

Another lovely Christmas over.

I felt horrible. JR was ticked at me too. He said my attitude made everyone uncomfortable. Are you kidding me? What about my level of discomfort?! Did anyone's attitude contribute to that at all? I

121

had no energy to argue so I just cried silently and eventually closed my eyes all the way home.

My ego was pleased. It was justified. I was a martyr.

Now that you have read my little Christmas nightmare, here is what I learned from it:

1. It is MY responsibility to care for myself.
2. I am not the judge of other people's attitude, or state of awareness.
3. The most important person in the room is me!
4. The same also goes for every single individual at any given time: each of us is the most important person in the room.

Let's look a little closer at the series of events as they could happen when I integrate these lessons:

Firstly, I could have had a talk with Amy weeks in advance and asked her to arrange a sleepover. Then, I could have taken the responsibility of insuring that I could discretely get up and take rests during the meal, in between courses, in order to avoid a meltdown. I could have let go of my insecurities concerning the fact that I was not included in the kitchen as Amy's mother. I could have chosen to appreciate that these people like my daughter and wanted to help her make a great meal. I also could have asked that gift giving be arranged so that we could get our side of the family done by 10pm. And, if not sleeping over, by 10 pm, finished or not, I could have wished everyone a good night and JR and I could have left without putting a damper on the party.

The most important person in the room is each of us.

This way of looking at things may seem selfish but it is quite the contrary. When you are serenely enjoying the company of others, you are being considerate. It is a mark of respect to those around you when you take good care of yourself, when you allow yourself whatever it takes to make the moment as pleasant as possible for you. You are worthy. You possess the ability to shine and spread joy around!

Chapter 9

Staying

The new year of 2011 began quietly. JR and I went out to brunch on the 1st. We talked as usual, watched movies and played games on the computer. Everything seemed normal. I got a flare-up after Christmas for about five days and another one after New Year. JR spent a lot of time in his office, on his computer while I rested in bed. Because we were both light sleepers, we had opted for separate bedrooms and would make the occasional visit when the stars aligned.

I had a TV in my room, so we would watch movies in my bed when I was too tired to sit up. But somehow, while I was struggling to change my state of awareness, while I worked on healing, JR and I were drifting apart and I didn't notice.

Before I knew it, my world had changed forever.

I sensed that JR didn't feel right. He is an introvert when it comes to sharing feelings (men!), so I was used to investigating and interrogating until he expressed whatever was bothering him. We always talked through our issues or anything else weighing on our mind and our relationship was truly harmonious. During that particular period of time, I had been feeling poorly, so I figured he was just a bit down because of it.

I realised one day that it was always me going over to his bed to have a lie down together, for a nap or a talk, or just to cuddle. He no longer came into my room. One morning, I walked into his room and sat at the edge of his bed. He was lying down, eyes closed, but I knew he wasn't asleep. I asked him how he was feeling. He looked up, 'Tired', he said. I put my hand on his solar plexus area and asked: 'What is going on *here?*' as I applied a bit of pressure toward his heart. He closed his eyes again and I knew something was terribly wrong. His face had a sad, almost gloomy expression. It took another fifteen minutes before he finally told me what was on his mind.

Just before the Holidays, JR had been contacted on Facebook by his first love. The woman now lived in Germany where she had a very successful career. They began emailing each other occasionally and things evolved to where they were in daily communication. She was sending pictures of her self and they both recalled how much they had meant to each other. As the days went by, he was spending his evenings online with her and they "fell in love" all over again! She went so far as to tell him that she would buy him a plane ticket so they could be together again and rekindle their romance. She was offering him a life of luxury and passion.

I was so shocked that I barely responded to his confession. He said he still loved her and was going to be with her. He cried, as he felt so bad for me, ill and all alone. He said he would give me time to get things organised to move.

I did not react.

When I was finally able to speak, I asked about the fact that he told me 'I love you' every day. That was a lie! 'You are a liar and a cheater!' I said calmly (Thank heaven for Xanax). He said he loved me, just not in the same way he loved her. 'Gee', I said, 'you think? The woman is pure fantasy! You haven't seen her in forty years and you are ready to throw away a real relationship, a really good relationship, for a woman who is no longer the girl from your past?'

He closed his eyes again. Told me he was torn; didn't know what to do, was very sad.

I went back to my room and closed the door. I lay down and looked at the ceiling, my mind racing, my heart broken. I felt crushed physically and emotionally. Xanax can only do so much... I looked at my spiritual images and a great peace came over me.

I rested for some time until a soft knock at the door told me JR wanted to enter. He was asking about supper and house stuff. I told him to do whatever he wanted and that I didn't care in the slightest what that would be. Anger rose in me and I sat up and told him he could stop feeling so sad for me. 'I've been through hell and back' I said, 'I don't need you to get my stuff together and move out; I don't need you for anything. I will survive this. Go away; the sight of you makes me want to puke!' He stood there and took it without responding. 'You have betrayed me, I added, and hurt me and I want nothing to do with you!'

Brave man, he entered the room and sat at the edge of my bed. He told me that he had not *really* decided to go to Germany to be with her. He repeated that he still loved me. 'I don't trust you anymore and your words mean nothing; you two cheaters deserve each other.' I said, 'Neither one of you gave any thought or respect to the fact that you are in a committed relationship. Go away!' JR got up a walked out. I got up and slammed the door. I cried until I fell asleep. I woke up around suppertime. I fed Jessie and took her out. Came back and fixed myself a quick meal that I took back to my room without a look or a word to JR.

I watched TV in my room with my dog and slept relatively well that night. Then I woke to the overwhelming pain I was feeling throughout my whole being. I cried again for a while and got out of bed to take care of Jessie and myself. JR was in his office. I didn't care. I ate, washed, dressed, made my bed and laid on it for another day of misery.

Around eleven, JR walked in and stood at the end of my bed with his hands on his hips and declared that I was the woman for him and that he wanted to be with me.

You would think that this would make a girl jump for joy. Not!

His body language made me want to throw something at him but I barely acknowledged what he said. I told him that I was under whelmed by this declaration of his undying love for me, that he broke my heart, broke my trust and that I now had to decide if *I* wanted *him* in **my** life. I told him I needed time to think, to see if I could find it in me to forgive him and trust him again. I said that it was highly unlikely; that he had killed our love. He started tearing up and moved toward me. I asked him to go away and tell it to what's her name in Germany.

I wallowed in anger and self pity for a couple of days, refusing to have anything to do with him. I still loved him of course and I wanted to forgive him.

But how to rebuild trust?

Without trust, there can be no loving relationship. I needed to find a way back to trust. I decided the best way to start was for him to be totally transparent. So, I walked into his office and demanded to see their exchanged emails. He looked panic stricken. 'Yes, I want to see the love letters and everything. You want to fix us, this is the beginning: truth'. He refused, saying it would needlessly hurt me and turned off his computer. Hurt me. Ha! As if the damage wasn't already done. When he left for work, I opened the computer that we shared only to find that his session now had a password. I was livid. I knew that password must have been there for weeks and felt yet again, betrayed, discarded and unwanted.

I insisted once more the next day and he let me see some of the emails he and "she" had exchanged. He had cleaned out his files and kept none of the love letters. What I saw was perfectly innocent and I despised them both for it. I was bitchy and spared no energy to spread my bad mood around while JR, in his effort to fix us, was patiently weathering the storm he had brewed up.

I lay in bed day after day going over all the scenarios that involved me leaving him, moving out on my own again. I walked a fine line between exhaustion and total flare-up. I was scared and so, so very hurt. The man I loved did not love me anymore. This, most of all, caused me a new, more intense level of suffering. I had put all my trust, all my hopes for the future in this man and he had pulled the rug from under my already unsteady feet!

He would come in my room sometimes, and very emotionally assure me that he had realised how foolish he had been, that I was an exceptional woman and that he wanted to spend the rest of his life with me. He wanted to cuddle and kiss me but I wouldn't let him touch me, knowing full well that it would have provoked a deluge of tears that I did not want to let out in front of him just then.

I had many long phone conversations with Sandra, the only person I confided-in at the time regarding this situation. She helped me sort out my feelings and make some sense of it all. She was an angel!

And then a few days later, I made a decision that changed the course of my life. I took the first steps onto a path previously unknown to me; it presented me with the opportunity I had been so desperately longing to find for so long.

I was calmly meditating after looking at my spiritual pictures to connect with the Universe, the Light. Thoughts were slowly drifting past my mind when I closed my eyes and entered a calm and soothing state of awareness. And then one thought stood front and center: Throughout my life, in every circumstance that caused me even the smallest upset, I *always* reacted as a victim does to survive: with fear.

Fight or Flight. As I had fuelled my fears over decades, I had burnt out my body.

I knew from my number of enlightened readings that there are only two emotions at the root of all other emotions: Love and fear. It was clear for me at this moment that fear was familiar and that's why

I instinctively – and subconsciously - chose it every time without hesitation. But what did fear ever do *for* me? When had it ever served me aside from quickly putting on the car breaks at the right moment on the road? Fear, I realised, had always led me to the same place: grief, pain, despair...

What would happen, I wondered, if just once, I chose love instead? What did I have to lose? I already knew where fear would lead; what could be worse?

I sat up and looked at the beautiful images on my wall. I made a commitment to myself: I choose love!

No more tragedy.
No more drama.
From now on, I choose love.
I love this man.

He is flawed just like the rest of us and I could embrace the fact that he made a terrible mistake for reasons only known to himself at that point. I was going to believe that he truly regretted hurting me and I was going to forgive him and learn to trust him again.

I got up and walked to his office. I sat down and took his hands in mine. What followed was something very surreal as I opened my heart to him and swept away any doubt that we were meant to be together and that we would get through this. I told him that we both would have to work hard to rebuild our relationship and he was totally on board with that. I asked that he permanently sever his communications with that woman. He asked me to stay as he wrote her a final word of goodbye. He wrote that what they had experienced was a mere fantasy – due on his part, to his lack of self-esteem, - that he loved me deeply and regretted hurting me so badly.

I read the email and he wrapped his arms around me as he sent the message. A huge, deep sorrow welled up inside me and I began to cry as we held on to each other. He repeated over and over that he was sorry, so very sorry. We both cried. When I calmed down, I got up and told him that major repair was to be done on our relationship. 'I love you' he said. The trust was gone. No amount of *I love you* was going to fix this. So, I responded thus: 'You said it to another woman. It means nothing to me now. If you do love me, then your actions will have to do the talking for you. Until I trust you, and it may take a very long time until I do, please don't say these words to me again.'

JR was totally committed to fixing our relationship. We embarked on a journey of discovery. Once again, I used my life-coaching tools, which we would put to good use. We eventually made a vision board and a vision statement for our relationship; we worked many hours on putting words to paper, both private and shared thoughts and realisations. We identified our values, our wants and needs, and the precise actions we were prepared to take to make our life together happy and fulfilled. This reunification process took many months. It was worth every minute.

We learned a lot of important things about our own self and about each other. We began to say Grace out loud before lunch every day, as we took time to be truly grateful for all the blessings in our life. Love filled our hearts and our home. By the time summer came around, we were closer than we had ever been.

When I look back, I see that JR needed to feel special and manlier, and I realise that I had not tuned into that need before. He realised that it was his responsibility to fulfill his needs and it was mine to be helpful and supportive of his life choices. And vice-versa.

We discovered our new, shared life path and experienced a transformation that comes from letting your heart...*break open.*

For the first time in my life, I had stayed in the present moment without fighting or running from the pain.

Living in a state of openness and gratitude gradually became more natural for both of us. I don't remember the exact moment it happened, but I did forgive JR quite naturally. I learned to trust not just him, but life.

I began to let go of things I couldn't control and became more conscious of my worrying habit; something I had to release. After all, when has worrying ever made any situation better?

I learned that when you choose love, it lives in your every cell. No matter what direction my life would take, I could *always* choose love and remain on my chosen path.

What a wonderful thing it is to know that there always are countless joys to choose from on this journey that is life!

Listening

When challenges came up, I now decided that I would choose to simply throw love at them, do what I can do, and observe how everything happens naturally, just the way it is meant to happen. That in itself would prove to be a challenge for my ego but I was determined. Yep, I would love the dragon too...

I began paying attention to my body at a more profound level. Was I feeling tension somewhere in my back? Then I needed to ask myself why; to ask my body what it wanted me to know. If the answer didn't manifest itself right away, I would breathe-in Love. After all, it is everywhere in the universe and is available at all times; one just needs to become conscious of it because the very nature of Love is consciousness. I learned to become the observer in the *now*. Everything didn't necessarily need fixing; it needed to be experienced. I began to really *listen* to my body, my mind and my soul.

Joy filled me every day and spiritual messages, or intuitions if you will, began to surface in my consciousness. A new perspective rose from the deep-rooted pain I had experienced most of my life. I realised that my childhood couldn't have been without some moments of joy shared with my parents. My mother must have cared for me or else I would have died. Babies need a lot of care! Even if a mother is overwhelmed or not particularly adept, she, and the father must have given some of themselves if their baby survived while in their care.

That thought led me to look at the milestones that I had built into the story of my life. My happy childhood memories were mostly about my grandfather who passed away when I was five years old. He lived in the country where I could be in touch with nature and when I was with him, I knew my parents could not bother me. All other milestones were sad and painful events involving one or both my parents. When my parents divorced, my father exited my life. I was 9. In my eyes, my mother became the "bad guy" on her own while he slowly faded from my consciousness. Part of me missed my dad, but a bigger part of me was relieved from having to deal with his harmful and unhealthy behaviour toward me.

So the path of my life until young adulthood was bleak to say the least. But now, I wondered if the pain, anger and resentment I had harboured since then had tainted my memories and totally eclipsed some that may have been happy. I began to visualise my path and I realised that there was a lot of space between the milestones. What was in those spaces? Could there be other, unnoticed mileposts that represented events that were not all sadness and fear?

During my rest periods, I worked a long time to visualize the child I had been. She was walking on the path and she stopped to feel the happy events of her life. The times when her mother was pleased with her, took her shopping or let her try on her high-heeled shoes. There were also times when she and her mother laughed together as they ate chunks of orange cheddar cheese. Each unearthed happy memory was now a new landmark. I continued until I could see that my journey was filled with different shades and colors that I could choose to look at between the old, sombre milestones. There was a new light shining on my life. There was now an opportunity to focus on the bright side.

As I was growing up, I made friends easily and I was often the teacher's pet because I loved to learn and read. So, school was a place where I had wonderful experiences. Playing outside with my friends got me into all kinds of adventures. And, as a teenager, I had the time of my life with some of the best people I have ever known. By the time I had reviewed my life's journey, many more landmarks were shining along a path that no longer seemed so dark.

The combination of having chosen to stay with JR, along with this new, more profound aspect of self-discovery brought me to a point where I was ready to forgive my mother completely. I was finally able to let go and forgive. I quite naturally and easily gave up passing judgment on my mother. I was releasing myself from a need to be right, to be the victim, to be faultless in my suffering for so long. What ever my mother had done in her life, I was now at peace with the understanding that her actions stemmed from her unique state of consciousness.

We are all human, flawed and fragile, strong and fine. *All of us embody what we are and circumstances are what they are*: this thought is the essence of non-judgement, of peace within one self. Letting things be, those matters that are beyond our control, is a very freeing state of mind.

I picked up the phone one day and called my mother. I told her that I wanted to give her my phone number. She asked if she had my permission to use it... I told her that I would be happy to talk to her if she agreed to leave the past in the past and if she agreed to not criticise me or anyone that I love. She, of course was very emotional. In her mind, she was the wounded party and had no idea why I had treated her so badly over the years. My mother knew quite naturally how to push my buttons. I listened with as much compassion as I could muster and when I'd had enough, I firmly and nicely put an end to the call. I was amazed to notice that I had a lesser need to be defensive!

I was at a place where I knew who I was a bit more and no longer gave anyone the power to define me. Not even my mother. It did take a few months and a few difficult conversations for my mother and I to begin to move forward in our relationship. I invited her over for lunch on a day when JR was at work and it was pleasant enough. She then had both of us over for lunch at her home. JR and she got on well. It was the first time that my mother had ever approved of any man in my life. It made things easier and would give us all a chance at a new beginning.

To this day, when I have interactions with my mother, I need to remember my commitment to non-judgment (It really does take lots of practice!) and to simply breathe. And listen. We all need to be heard and it is a gift that I am able to offer her most of the time, without too much expenditure of energy.

Chapter 10

Gratitude, Gratitude, Gratitude!

I often refer to our body as our "ride"; and it is obvious that we best take good care of it if we want to travel this earth for a long time. In the 1970s, I was a regular at a tiny local health food store and became increasingly aware that what we choose to fuel our body and spirit is of considerable importance. I took to studying books on nutrition and began to get interested in yoga, meditation and eastern spiritual philosophy.

How then, could I get such an all-consuming and disabling illness at age 46?

I believe that I had overlooked one vital element that is essential for health: Beautiful thoughts. Ever since I decided to walk on a path of healing, this dimension becomes clearer every day. I had now learned the true essence of forgiving, first through my experience with JR. Forgiving him gave me sufficient awareness to release myself from the bonds of resentment and allow myself to forgive my mother. Those two events radically changed my outlook on life. I became more at peace with myself. I liked myself more, not in an egotistical 'I'm always right' sort of way, but in saying to myself: 'Hey, you did good today; I'm proud of you.'

I have been a long-time admirer of Louise Hay and Dr Christiane Northrup. I had attempted on several occasions to put their teachings into concrete actions but I obviously wasn't ready until now. This was the time when I actually could communicate to my body and to my self, that I was loved. Really, really, loved. By me!

In time, it was becoming quite natural for me to pass by a mirror and say: 'Hello, gorgeous!' I had even graduated to the doctorate level – as Louise Hay calls it – of taking time to look into my own eyes in the mirror and say out loud: 'I love you. I really, really love you!'

This led me to a new appreciation of my ride. I would regularly take a few minutes when dressing or getting ready for a bath to stand in front of a mirror and just look at my body. Without judgment. I looked and marvelled at this wondrous machine that still marched on in spite of overwhelming adversity.

Of course, my ego was trying to override this fresh train of thoughts. How on earth could I love this almost 60 year-old body when I didn't even appreciate the great body I was fortunate enough to have had in my 20's and 30's? I had cellulite and fat calves, my belly was flabby and my chin was too small and gave the impression that I had two of them, and, and, and, yet...

I loved this body for it had managed to survive a serious illness and it still strived to heal. I grasped the notion that my body was enduring, resilient and beautiful, warts and all! My body deserved respect and tenderness, kindness too. I began to regularly say to this body that had bore my children and served me so well: 'I thank you and honour you for all that you have done for me'.

I showed appreciation for my body by becoming more conscious of its needs for stretching, walking in the fresh air, pacing, resting, breathing deeply, etc. I showed my body respect with my thoughts and also by providing it with higher quality supplements, clean water and the most nutritious organic foods I could afford.

I made it my mission to transform my body into a sanctuary of peace. Lots to do!

Or *not* do? Hmmm.

Now almost fifteen years old, Jessie's health was seriously deteriorating. She was almost blind and had a heart murmur that now caused her increased distress. After a last Christmas with my family to give every one a chance to say their goodbyes, I made the heart-breaking decision to put an end to her life. Less than two weeks later, in February of 2012, I began to have heart issues, which I had experienced at a lesser degree in previous years. This time, the erratic heart rate and the tightness in my chest was much more intense and JR drove me to the hospital. I was immediately rushed to the emergency ward and a heart monitor was put on me along with other paraphernalia. The cardiologist told me that she was admitting me as soon as a bed became available. I stayed in the emergency ward for 36 gruelling hours of bright lights, loads of noise and naturally, an abundance of sick people!

What worried me - and the doctors having no clue as to the nature of my illness, I had to manage this myself – is that with a deficient immune response, I was extremely vulnerable to viruses and being around this great number of flu patients was dangerous for me because the slightest cold could result in my being bed bound for weeks. JR brought me dark glasses to protect my over-sensitive eyes from the brutal neon lights, earplugs and a cloth with my essential oils to repel viruses and bacteria.

Still, I couldn't sleep a wink day or night and my heart was pounding louder and harder. I told the attending doctor that it was imperative to isolate me as far as possible from the action of the ER. I explained again about ME and told him that I actually may not survive another night without sleep. A few minutes later, I was taken to a closed-off area of the emergency ward, away from everybody. By the time my daughters came to visit, I was resting at last. A nurse came by and told us that there was a room for me and that I would be taken up. I was so relieved! The girls put everything on my gurney, on top of me, and I was wheeled into a semi-private room in the geriatric ward.

I won't go into my weeklong stay at the hospital. Suffice it to say that it was pretty horrible. The staff was nice but they were so overworked that they couldn't meet the needs of their patients. Our health system is defective as are many around the world.

My cardiologist sent me to a big city hospital for an induced cardiac stress test. An ambulance took me there and a private nurse accompanied me. We were gone for most of the day. I got up only to go to the bathroom. When my turn came, I was wheeled into a small room where no less than three cardio specialists waited to poke at me and plug me into all sorts of equipment... Then I was given a shot of a drug that increased my heart rate as if I was running. As this was happening, one doctor swept an ultrasound instrument around my chest area and all three doctors were looking at a large TV-like screen, taking notes, conferring. When my heart rate reached a certain point, I became agitated and had difficulty breathing in spite of the reassurance I was given that all was well and that I was doing great.

I couldn't believe the pain and thought my heart would explode! I was thinking that this had to be dangerous for my delicate condition and I went into that zone, you know, the 'I don't care' what happens now... I drifted into a different kind of consciousness and for some reason, felt the need to look up and at the right side, behind my head. What I saw was the most wondrous thing I have ever contemplated.

There, on the screen, was a surprisingly vivid image of my own heart beating hard and fast. It was bigger than life and filled with bright colors. I could see the blood swishing in and out. In that moment, I felt no pain, no worry. The beauty of my magnificent, strong and luminous heart awed me into a calm and grateful state. The test was over before I knew it. The doctors slipped the results in an envelope, which they handed to my nurse and back we went into the ambulance. I asked the nurse to look at the results. She opened the envelope and showed me the report as she explained the medical terms. Turns out my heart was not working at optimal capacity but there was no pathology or apparent reason for my problems. I guess ME *not being apparent* makes it OK. Right.

I will never forget that image of my heart and to this day, when I close my eyes and feel my beautiful heart beating with might, it fills me with gratitude and much, much love. I know that I must use my heart as a beacon of love so that it keeps beating with joy. As I meditate, I feel love for my heart and when I feel it radiating with love, I let my heart turn into a bright light that sends out love to all that is.

Yes, our beautiful body is wondrous beyond our understanding.

Once I settled back home after my stay in hospital, it felt so good to sleep in darkness and without interruptions. Needless to say that I had missed JR and the simple, healthy homemade food that we enjoyed together. I felt clean and so happy to be in my own environment!

Before releasing me from the hospital, my cardiologist was very understanding and forthcoming about the fact that he knew nothing about my illness and it's effect on my heart. On my request, he referred me to a colleague who practiced closer to home and that I would have to see once a year just to keep an eye on things. I was never told about the test results, other that everything was fine. Nothing to worry about...

I was enjoying my homecoming by spending my days in front of the TV or on my laptop, or sleeping. I felt calm and I was resting. All was well enough. My heartbeat had almost gone back to its *normal* rhythm.

One afternoon, JR answered the doorbell and was asked to sign a registered letter. That was enough to send my heartbeat into frenzy. Never, in all my life have I received good news by registered mail and this was no exception. The letter was to inform us that our landlords were repossessing our apartment at the end of our lease, which was 6 months away. I was very upset at the thought of moving once again so soon after settling in and I couldn't imagine finding the strength to do so. JR was upset too but took things calmly, as it is in his nature to do.

We had moved-in a mere 17 months ago; how could they do this! I had been very specific with our landlords concerning my health issues and our desire to stay there at least three years, so why were they not honest enough to tell us of their eventual plans before renting us the apartment? Why rent to us if they intended to move in after so short a time? How could they be so uncaring as to just send a letter, when they lived downstairs from us? My brain was going a hundred miles an hour with all these questions that did nothing to solve my problem.

Worrying NEVER makes things better...

It took days for me to calm down and accept the situation. As I've mentioned before, people with ME have a very difficult time managing stress and all that it triggers in their already overstressed body. How can one manage a dragon when one feels so weak and so overwhelmed? The answer to that question can only be found when we calm down our thoughts. Our brain needs to be refocused, not on the problem but again, on the simple act of breathing!

Focussing on breathing every single day, no matter what is going on in our life can, in time, make a difference between suffering and calmly handling the challenges that come up.

This first step is essential if we are to transcend illness, that is, go beyond the old and useless beliefs of being a *victim*.

As I slowly breathed in my bed, I started to take stock of the moment, to feel my whole being, to love it, to forgive my momentary lapse into panic. Peace descended upon me and at last, I began to see the bigger picture. In reality, JR wanted to retire from teaching at the music school and I wanted to move back home to the mountains. We both envisioned a peaceful life in beautiful surroundings and with nice, supportive neighbours. We had made our vision board and we had stayed focussed on manifesting our heart's desire. We gave thanks everyday for all that comprised our life together.

It was plain as the nose on my face that being forced to leave our apartment opened up a whole new realm of possibilities that would bring us to the manifestation of our vision! When JR and I talked about this in the light of the simple truth that *everything* is a present, we decided to go up north and look for a place to live. He would keep his teaching job on Saturdays only. We would manage by living in a smaller, less expensive place.

I had the idea that a mobile home could be a good solution to suit our budget, and we could even buy one with very little cash down. JR wasn't too keen on the idea but I showed him some pictures I found online and he warmed to the notion. There were wonderful places in the mountains with full services, lovely neighbourhoods and nearby lakes. A month after my stay in the hospital, we began sorting our belongings once more. I started packing away a few boxes of winter clothing. Then, one day, while surfing the Internet, I found the perfect mobile home located in just the right area. We looked at the pictures and made arrangements to go up north. As long as we were making the trip there, we also made plans to visit a lower duplex apartment within our means. We went there first and we really didn't like it all that much. It was far from the highway but not far enough; we could hear the sound of traffic from the balcony. I desperately wanted to hear nothing but the sound of nature, most and foremost.

When we arrived at the mobile home, we discovered a clean, well-groomed neighbourhood. The house itself was nice but didn't have much of a view at all. We felt an immediate affinity with the lady who owned the mobile home park, which included access to the nearby lake and to the swimming pool for all the residents. It was a quiet community. The house itself was nice, but a bit too old; we didn't want to have to invest into and live through repetitive repairs. We had a lovely visit, met her husband and were getting ready to leave when the lady said they had an apartment to rent in a newly built house. It was their family home and she wasn't advertising the lower duplex apartment because she wanted to choose her tenants. She liked us.

We all drove up to a gorgeous, modern wooden house on the slope of a magnificent mountain. It offered a breathtaking view. We had to climb stairs to get up to the ground floor apartment. As soon as we walked through the door, we were struck by the brightness of the space. No wonder; there were wall-to-wall windows in the kitchen/living area and we could see for miles across a valley surrounded by numerous other mountains. It was my dream come true. The bedroom and office area were in the back of the apartment. A semi-basement, but still surprisingly well lit thanks to large windows. We loved this place but the price the owners were asking for rent was a bit high for us. We told them we would think about it.

It was obvious that the lady wanted us as much as we wanted the place. To my astonishment, as we started down the long stairway, JR turned around and asked if they would take $50 off the rent and in just a few seconds, they said OK. Amazing! If you knew JR, you'd know that as an introvert, it is really not in his nature to do something so bold.

Funny how life works: Very often, you just have to ask for what you want.

We drove back home elated and excited about moving. We even asked our landlords if they would let us out of our lease 3 months earlier and they accepted. I asked for that in writing... We went back up north to sign the new lease and take measurements, and by June we were in our new home.

I had moved a total of 5 times between 2005 and 2013; this was my third with JR, so you could say that I was getting good at it. I managed everything at a pace that would keep me from flaring but as you can imagine, it was very difficult and I was constantly pushing my energy envelope. But by the time the moving truck drove away, I felt the energy of the mountains that I so loved and knew that they would help me to heal. JR, who had lived in the city all his life, discovered that being surrounded by nature was very much to his liking.

Our upstairs landlords turned out to be lovely neighbours with two well-behaved children. The house was so well constructed that we are hardly aware that someone is living upstairs. We've become friendly with the whole family and occasionally sit on the outside stairs for a chat. We had previously told the owners that I would eventually want another dog and it was OK with them when I assured them that it would be a small one and that I would train it well. Besides, I'm almost always home, so they knew the dog wouldn't be left alone very often.

On June 7th, I told JR that I was ready for a dog and that it would be a rescue, female, and that her name would be Luna (for one of my favourite Harry Potter characters). After essentials were unpacked, I began checking out the local SPCA and other shelters online. I wanted a small non-shedding dog. I must have looked at hundreds of pictures of cute dogs needing a home; many had been named Luna. On the morning if July 1st, I turned on my laptop and immediately went on the local SPCA site. There, looking at me was a 2 year-old Yorkie mix named Luna. I knew I had found my dog.

As I write these words, she sleeps near me on the sofa, opening an eye once in a while to check on me. The fascinating thing about this is that Luna was actually her real name at birth and not one given by the shelter as they usually do with strays. An elderly woman who had found her too difficult to handle gave up this little girl. If you know anything about Yorkshire Terriers, you know that they can be very bossy and stubborn. I knew what to expect and had no problem training this clever furry angel. JR however, is another story. Basically, he loves Luna and she does boss him around quite often, but as time goes by, he is affirming himself not just with her, but in general.

More than ever before, JR and I count our blessings and give thanks every day. Whenever something bothers me, I often take stock *in the moment*. If I have negative thoughts, I remind myself that there is no tragedy in my life, no drama: everything is a gift.

It takes work and discipline to live in a state of grace, if not all of the time, then some of the time. But it is possible to envision and manifest our heart's desire. It is possible to wake up in the morning and say a silent "'Thank You" for all the blessings in our life.

Chapter 11

Loving

JR proposed and gave me my first-ever engagement ring on Valentine's Day 2013, shortly after my hospital stay and before the move. I said yes to marriage for the third time. I do believe in it and I'm going to get it right this time if it's the last thing I do. I feel that this is right and I know it because I have sharper and more profound insights than ever before; I can feel the difference in the way I handle myself. I am now not so quick to panic or to judge; important factors that remove much stress from my life.

A fresh start in beautiful new surroundings was a very good sign that the universe was conspiring with us.

After the move, I did experience flare-ups, but I remained calm, remembered to breathe and just let my body do what it needed to do. I noticed that my energy level didn't dip quite as low as it had in the past. I was mostly in bed for the duration which was now usually 5 days, or so. Something more had shifted inside of me and that something was allowing me to stabilise my condition. On days when I paced myself, I felt better. Other days were just exhaustion and pain, but whatever I was experiencing, it was with a sense of grace. A sense that I was healing in a more profound way than ever before, so it became easier to let go and, yes, let God.

Grocery days are still the worse and I'm so lucky to have JR to do the heavy lifting. We share household tasks – I cannot even *look* at a vacuum cleaner – and we do get along famously. I feel that the time we spend together offers us a new, more conscious connection. We listen more to our own heart and open up to each other. We touch more and have become much, much closer than I could ever have imagined. No, we have not become oversexed like teenagers again, but our closeness has taken several dimensions. We are simply, quietly, gently, happily in love.

This kind of loving is a new experience for me. I find that my heart has opened to love and can embrace the whole world. When I am in this new state of awareness and able to manage my ego, I can actually feel love pouring out of me. So, I practise this as I rest. I feel the love coming from the universe and I connect with it. It is a most uplifting sensation. I find it impossible to stay depressed or stressed when I can go deep inside myself and connect with love. Of course, as I mentioned before, this does take practise but over time, it is something you can do whenever you wish, in any situation. Really, whatever the problem is that you are struggling with; just *throw love at it* and you'll see things get better. What have you got to lose?

Nothing but love: That's what I want in life and I do my best to remember that. This has made me realise that there really are *no* problems; only challenging experiences that can either make us grow in love or in fear... It's up to us.

I choose love. Always. Now as for my ego, well, I need to keep working on getting it to cooperate!

In August of 2013, JR and I were married in the lovely garden of my mother's house. Family and close friends formed a loving circle around us. It was a perfect day and my energy level was pretty good. Naturally! This was a day of re-unification for my family as, for the first time, my mother really was *mother* of the bride. As soon as she found out about our engagement, she insisted on giving us a wedding. She took care of everything. I barely lifted a finger for the preparations. I ordered my dress online, had it taken in a bit and it looked pretty good. My daughters and their boyfriends helped out along the way and on the day of the wedding. We had the most beautiful and delicious wedding cake and even the weather was perfect.

Who would have thought that choosing love over fear would bring me such an overabundance of joy?

I think back on that day when JR was leaving me and I remember asking myself: 'What if, for once, I chose love'? And I realise that choosing love is simply choosing our self, our own happiness. Putting that before our grievances is an act of love towards others as well. There is no downside to choosing love. It solves an innumerable amount of issues and difficulties when we put it into action; after all, love is a verb.

Fabulous me

As previously mentioned, people living with chronic illness tend to be self-centered. If anyone has an issue with that, then until they have to live with a dragon, 24/7, I really think they should keep it to themselves.☺ Those of us who do have to manage a constant presence of fierce proportions know that trying to explain our situation is often an exercise in futility. It is a sad state of affairs when we do our best to describe what our life is like and are frequently subjected to disbelief, indifference and humiliation from health professionals, friends and even relatives. When our illness goes on for years, people get bored and tell us they're tired of hearing about it. 'What's new?' they ask, but they don't want to know. Not much happens on a day-to-day basis for the most part as our life revolves around the dragon.

We are not being *positive* when we lie about how badly we feel, nor are we *negative* when we do talk honestly about our symptoms. I'm not referring to whining and ranting on and on, I'm simply stating that there is something healthy about standing in our truth when interacting with *normals*, as we like to call healthy folks.

It is essential however, to keep in mind that waiting for recognition is not going to make it happen. Besides, we do not need recognition from anyone but our own self. So, again, we must ignore our ego or keep it in line with the program, which is to recognise and embrace our own worth.

Affirmations (as per Louise Hay) are the most effective tools I have found for raising my awareness of my own magnificence. As I'd done before, I kept on with deliberately taking the time to appreciate my body and to tell myself sweet things in front of the mirror, but now I needed to take it a step further.

Dr Christiane Northup has a show on Hay House Radio called *Flourish*. When I first read that term, I associated it with the journey to self; it deeply resonated for me. This is where I was on my personal trek. I held a vision in my mind and in my heart, where I walked on my path of healing with the intent of flourishing. This new vision brought me to the understanding that I was *allowed* to shine and that it was high time I learned to do so in my own way, without focussing on my limitations.

I added a new series of affirmations that I repeated several times a day. I strengthened my intent to flourish by including praise in my inner dialogue, catching myself whenever I indulged in self-criticism.

Replacing a lifetime of devaluating thoughts by notions that empower us takes some effort. Fortunately it is not physically or mentally or even emotionally demanding. *Au contraire!* Real power is in the moment. It lies in stillness – as often do we... All it takes is attention or if you prefer, awareness, to change the way our mind works and to learn discipline and patience. Learning to be kind to our self can be daunting when we have been taught to keep our head down and that it is wrong to stand out.

Do NOT believe everything you think.

It is great to shine. Just imagine asking Byoncé or any of your favourite *stars.* We do not have to be famous or on a reality show to spread our wings and flourish, shine and be fabulous.

New on my bedroom mirror and on the pages of my agenda: I am fabulous!

When I first started, I didn't *really* believe my affirmations but in time, I began to feel more comfortable in my body. I felt more relaxed even if I became too tired or achy. I was experiencing a new peace and that peace was taking up residence in my cells.

Fabulous me!

It is good to shine!

Loving begins with self. Once love begins to flow freely through us, we can spread its light out into the world in whatever unique way we can.

Chapter 12

Living from the Heart

This is a short chapter. I invite you to complete it and make it your very own.

A handful of experts are working tirelessly around the world to find a cure for patients who, for the most part, are not receiving adequate medical care for this illness. I am one of them. The available treatments are encouraging in some cases but for most of us it is a long series of trial and error with doctors who have no clue of what they are dealing with.

I am still on my own with my dragon.
I tell myself to forget it.
Forget what I think I know.
Nobody's brain knows anything for sure, anyway.

Forget what my ego tells me. That, in itself is a full-time job unless I just forget it. Forget it.

Let it be.
Let it go.

And if there's one thing I would like you to take away from my story, it's this: It's OK to forget all that you have just read; only you, in your heart, know what best serves you and the world.

Listen.

Write you own unique insights and you will see a way to transcend the beliefs that no longer serve you.

Living from the heart. What does that mean, really? As I understand it, this is what happens when one lives from the heart: For example, an event occurs or you are faced with a decision and you are uncertain of the actions you want to take. You choose to put aside what your head tells you and you connect with your inner voice to find better solutions and an authentic way of expressing yourself in the world.

Living from the heart requires that I first become aware of the physical sensations that my heart is emitting. That is easy enough during a meditative or contemplative rest period.

The second step is letting myself *feel* the emotion that is coming from my heart center. This is particularly challenging when my ego is busy inventing a story that will raise my stress level by convincing me for example, that I am a victim of other people's actions. But taking a few deep breaths and just stepping back for a moment is sufficient for me to become aware of my heart's emotion.

All I have to do is listen, be present, be aware. Just breathe... and listen.

The simplicity of this may seem too good to be true or it may seem too difficult to achieve but it is in fact, extremely easy!

I know that discipline is not an appealing notion for people like us, but really, what is the downside of including a healing practise in your day; one that you can do as you are lying down? Just a few minutes a day here and there have changed my world.

Practicing *living from the heart* prepares me for situations and interactions with others. When things get sticky, I sometimes forget to keep still inside and listen to my heart while focussing on what the other person is saying. My ego usually gets ready to give a self-serving answer, so the real me remains silent because of my state of unawareness. Still, I eventually realise what has happened and endeavour to do better next time. Sometimes, I am truly present as I listen in awareness and it is sublime to really connect with someone. When this occurs, I am genuinely living from the heart and the outcome of a situation is the best it can be.

It is only at the heart level that such questions as: "Who am I?" can be answered. I have discovered that I am a spirit in a body of flesh and bones. I am a traveler on a learning expedition through time and space and I know that this earth life is but a fragment of my journey. You may not agree with my belief that I am a spirit having a human experience. That's fine. This is my own vision. Do find your own personal answer. Knowing who we are is essential to healing.

It is the essence of our whole *being* that defines us and not what we *do*. It is an empowering experience to say out loud: 'I am'! To affirm our real identity from the heart is saying that we matter, whatever limitations we may think we have.

As I delved more frequently into my heart's inner voice, I searched for things that could give my life meaning. What is my unique *talent*, I wondered, now that I am living with a dragon? Gone were the days when I fervently enjoyed acting, horseback riding, cycling and writing the screenplay that would change my life. Well, the script is completed and awaiting its day (or closer to the truth), waiting for me to gather my courage and find a way to pitch it! But again, I digress...

The consensus is clear: Our life has meaning when we express our passion and our uniqueness in a way that makes the world a better place – even if it's just our little corner of it. We can't all be Oprah or Bill Gates and that's fine. They serve the world in a way that suits them and their situation. We can look to them as role models and inspiration to find our own path to healing.

*Meaning **is** healing.*

I've found that writing gives my life meaning as does playing the guitar (although I'm not very good at it, yet). Taking care of my home with my husband makes life worthwhile too. I get satisfaction from caring for my little dog, from listening and sharing with a friend or giving solicited (well, not always ☺) advice to my grown children, and from hugging my grandchildren whenever possible. I love to help people and animals. I participate in support groups online and also sign petitions for causes that are important to me.

When I look at it like that, my life seems pretty full. And yet, I am mostly homebound with "you know who" and JR and Luna.

Living from the heart also means knowing our purpose. As I learned to listen to my inner voice, I began to wonder what my role was in this world. What I found may surprise you. It is my belief that we all, every single one of us have the exact same purpose: Receiving and giving joy.

Joy manifests in our heart from the awareness of our own being and of all that makes our life meaningful.

Rich or poor, healthy or sickly, young or old, everyone CAN give. If you have doubts, try this on for size: Breathe in. You have just received oxygen from mother earth. Breathe out. You have just paid it forward to her vegetation!

Living from the heart is the only path I know of, that leads to wellbeing and to the happiness that resides in the moment.

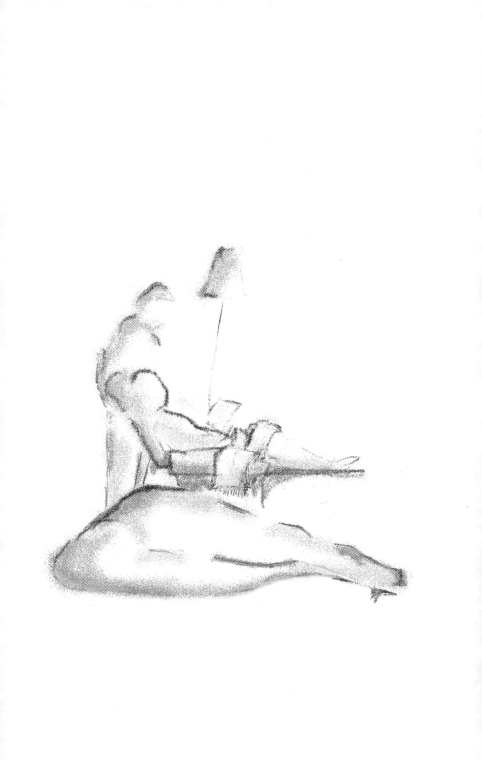

Afterword

Higher Maintenance

Living with chronic illness can be challenging at best but very discouraging when the going gets rough. At a time when the dragon seemed untameable, managing its unpredictable tantrums was a full-time job.

Yes, I am *high maintenance*, that's for sure. For 15 years, I have made healing a priority. Every day, I focussed on healing. I prayed for healing, asked the Universe for healing energy, visualised healing. I did everything in my power to heal!

But the dragon is still here with me... Although he does seem a bit smaller and better behaved. In spite of the fact and very likely *because* of the fact that I live with this illness, I have healed parts of my being that I probably would not have accessed before.

So, I have decided to let go of my focus on looking for THE cure and leave that up to the Universe. I have moved-on beyond the path of healing. I have transcended this illness in that it does not govern my life anymore.

Today, my focus is on living. I walk a path that is full of colours and infinite possibilities! It is a path that requires *Higher Maintenance*, meaning higher awareness and discipline. It is the path of the soul, the path of life. It is a life that does require me to be alert to the signs when my body speaks to me. I endeavour to always make the choices that will allow me to flourish, to enjoy the moment. If I do choose to participate in a gathering that I know will cost me loads of energy, then I go for it and accept that it may – or someday, may not... - cost me pain and major recuperation time. This is my life. This is life.

I began this book by stating that there is no magical recipe for a joyful life when you live with chronic illness.

Perhaps there is one after all.

It is a recipe that I believe can help us transcend all of life's challenges:

> I don't believe everything I think.
> I simply count my blessings and give thanks.

Thank you for reading. May you find joy each and every day.

We really *are* fabulous, so, let's go ahead and claim that without apology. Let us practice *Higher Maintenance* and shift our focus on living a life of infinite possibilities!

Resources

Here is my personal list of some of the works, groups, people and websites that have inspired me in my life and in the writing of this book. Whatever your specific condition may be, you can be sure that there are people out there who are experiencing the same issues and who will welcome, inform and support you.

- *butyoudontlooksick.com* - This website grew from the immensely popular *Spoon Theory*, (a must read for any person with a chronic illness) written and presented by the multi-talented Christine Miserandino.

- Hunter Hopkins Center's ME/CFS/FM is a Facebook group I like very much. It is run by dedicated people who provide a place where you will find support, information, humour and compassion.

- Fellow patient, Clarissa Shepherd's book, *Find Your Way: A Guide to Healing While Living with Chronic Fatigue Immune Dysfunction*

Syndrome and Fibromyalgia offers a wealth of useful information. Clarissa also created *Fellow Travelers,* a Facebook group that she runs with a kind and loving spirit.

- Tony Bernhard writes insightful articles in Psychology Today. She has also written books that can be helpful tools to work on Higher Maintenance.

- *cortJohnson.org* – Great website for the latest information. *Phoenix Rising* is "committed to providing ME/CFS and Fibromyalgia patients with up to date and accurate information on research, treatment and advocacy."

- Louise L. Hay. I can't say enough about this extraordinary woman who has done so much to help people live a healthier, happier life! Her best-selling book *You Can Heal Your Life* rarely leaves my night table. Her publishing company, HAY HOUSE, has assembled some of the best authors (many of my favourites) in the field of, you guessed it, Higher Maintenance. At *hayhouse.com,* you'll certainly find an approach that will help you further on your path of wellness.

- And here are some of Marianne Williamson's best quotes for a joyful life:
    1- Forgiveness is not always easy. At times, it feels more painful than the wound we suffered, to forgive the one that inflicted

it. And yet, there is no peace without forgiveness.

2- Miracles occur naturally as expressions of love. The real miracle is the love that inspires them. In this sense everything that comes from love is a miracle.

3- We ask ourselves, 'Who am I to be brilliant, gorgeous, talented, fabulous?' Actually, who are you not to be?

4- Love is what we were born with. Fear is what we learned here.

5- The new midlife is where you realize that even your failures make you more beautiful and are turned spiritually into success if you became a better person because of them. You became a more humble person. You became a more merciful and compassionate person.

6- The key to abundance is meeting limited circumstances with unlimited thoughts.

7- Joy is what happens to us when we allow ourselves to recognize how good things really are.

- I like the EFT technique. Nick Ortner has written books on the subject and given seminars all over the world. For more information on this easy and simple method to increase wellbeing, you can check out *thetappingsolution.com* or look up Nick on Youtube.

- If you are a woman of any age, Dr Christiane Northrup has published several books that celebrate our wondrous body by providing accurate medical information from a new and inspired perspective.

- Victor L. Frankl's book: *Man's Search for Meaning* is, in my humble opinion, one of the most profound books ever written.

- Bruce Lipton's book: *The Biology of Belief* is worth the energy it takes to read it. It will totally transform the way you look at life. *brucelipton.com*

- Kelly Howell has released several relaxation/ meditation CD's that I find very effective and enjoyable. There are several themes to choose from, including Healing. *brainsync.com*

- Eckhart Tolle's first book *the Power of Now* had an enormous impact on millions of people across the world. For more than a decade, *A New Earth* has been life transforming for countless readers, including myself. It also resides on my night table.

- The insightful book, *Zero Limits* (Featuring the ancient Hawaiian teachings of Ho'oponopono) by Joe Vitale and Ihaleakala Hew Len, PhD, offers a fascinating and effortless method to open the way to wellness in all aspects of life.

- The wonderful book, *Daring Greatly* by Brené Brown, Ph.D., LMSW, is one that will resonate with so many of us who need to appreciate vulnerability in our life and especially in our relationships.

• And finally, I want to include a work that is unknown to most and was written for serious seekers ONLY. It will either put-off or create great disturbance in one who is unconsciously clinging to intellectual notions and beliefs. So, proceed with an open heart or not at all because you'll be disappointed. This work transformed my life and made me question my faith and my place in the universe. But since 1987, it has turned out to be my greatest source of serenity. It is called: In the Light of Truth – *The Grail Message-__1931 Edition__*, by <u>Abdruschin</u>. (You may find a few versions of the same title online, without the specific edition date and with a variation in the spelling of the author's name. These are NOT the same original work, which is totally unaffiliated with groups or organizations.) This is an intensely spiritual work that is not affiliated with any *religion* nor does it ask the reader to give up his or her religion. You may not agree with its teachings. It is not my place to discuss, debate or defend its contents. *<u>http://www.abdrushin. us/in-the-light-of-truth/</u>*

Acknowledgements

I cannot thank my husband enough. He has participated in the creation of this book with correcting, editing and feedback. He is also responsible for building my website. But most of all, it is his faith in me and the countless hugs that fuelled my enthusiasm and kept me writing. I really do love you to the moon and back!

My sincere gratitude to my daughters, who provided precious help and resources to bring this project to fruition. You've been with me through the worst and asked so little in return. You are more precious to me than you'll ever know.

To my two best friends (you know who you are): Thank you for keeping me real during all these years. I cannot express the extent of my gratitude for the hours you've spent *being there* for me. To quote one of my favourite fictional characters (Spock): 'I have been, and always shall be, your friend'.

My deepest appreciation to the many people who, despite serious illness, share their resources and knowledge with their fellow patients by creating Facebook groups, blogs, articles and books. Your work makes a huge difference in the life of people who rely on you for the latest information, understanding, love and support. I also wish to thank all the wonderful members of online support groups who make up a caring community where we can rant, brag, make jokes and just be our self.

I wish to acknowledge the generosity of the following people whose financial support contributed to the manifestation of this book. I am eternally grateful!

Alexandre Salvas, Magda Badran,
Issa Lizon, Ryan Neral, Michel Blais,
Sophie Boulanger, Bianca Abbandonato,
Josée D'Amour, Sarah Vaiasicca,
Antoni Carlone, Carla Abbandonato,
Yves&Marie Cousineau, Bruce Murdoch,
Jean-Pierre Cousineau, Sharon Stewart.

My warmest thanks to my special dragon-taming friends:

Michele Krisko, Jacqueline Melzer,
Donni Lockridge, Claire Prideaux, Kathy Sayre,
Clarissa Shepherd and Rachael Allen.

Each of you has inspired, supported, and lifted me and countless others with your kindness, your insightful brilliance and loving presence.

Printed in the United States
By Bookmasters